# Gastric Sleeve Bariatric Cookbook for Beginners

"Discover your path to long-term wellness: 2000 days of irresistible, nutritious recipes for a healthy lifestyle after surgery.
Plus, Get a 21 Days Meal Plan as a Bonus!"

## Nancy Johnson

#### HEALTHY AND TASTY WITH
# Nancy

Hello dear reader, I sincerely hope that you had a pleasant experience with the book you just read. I am grateful for your decision to embark on this journey. Creating books is a hardworking process, and I strive to make each one special for you.

I would be immensely grateful if you could take some time to provide a review of this book. Your contribution is valuable and helps improve the content. Your kindness will be greatly appreciated, and for this reason, I thank you in advance for your time and support. Thank you!

Your Sincerly

*Nancy*

# Table of Contents

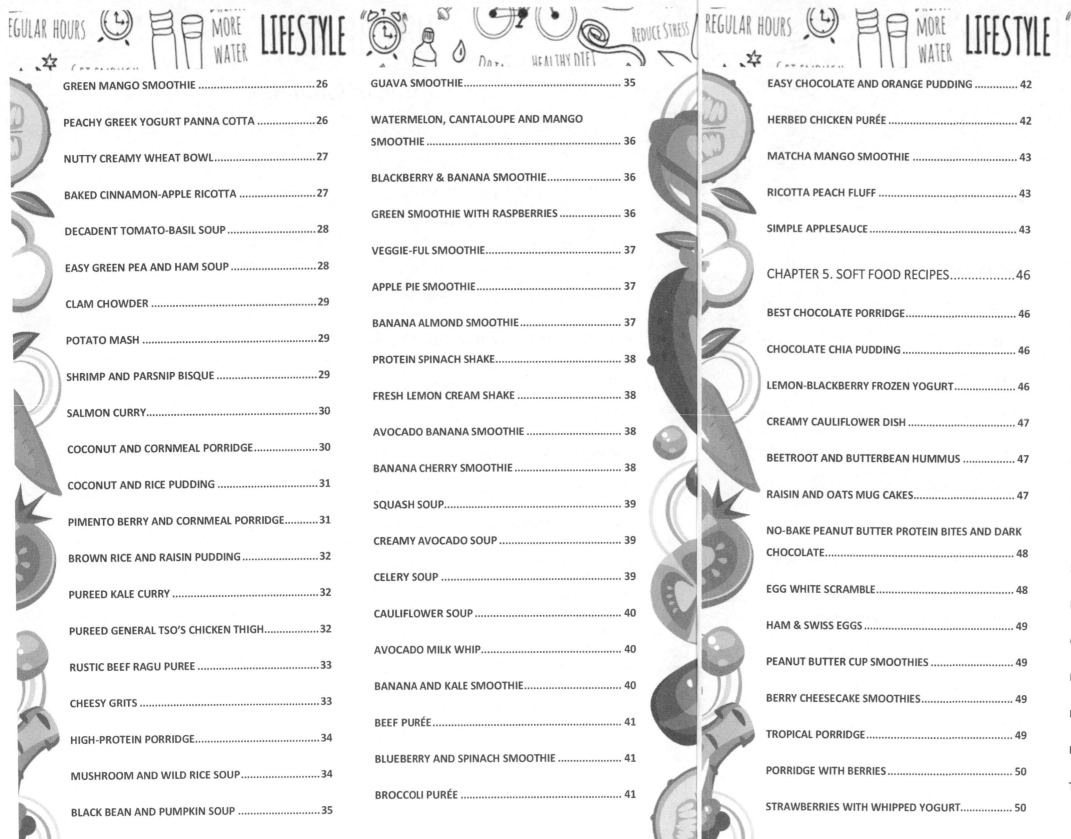

# Table of Contents

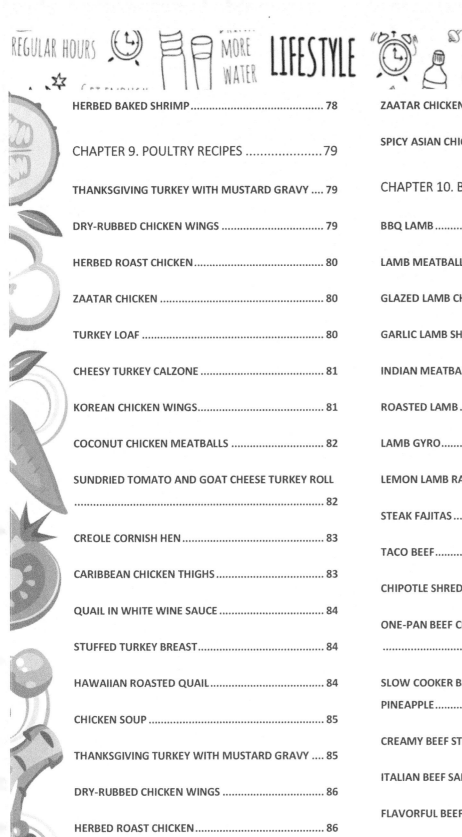

# INTRODUCTION

### The Comprehensive Gastric Sleeve Diet: Phases and Recommendations

The journey towards effective weight loss truly begins post-surgery. Following the surgical procedure, patients embark on a transformative path by adhering to a stringent diet. This dietary regimen aids in the body's recovery and adaptation to the altered stomach size. The fundamental principle of this diet involves consuming smaller, more frequent meals throughout one's lifetime. Although the stomach's capacity for food is reduced, quick consumption leads to the necessity of more frequent eating. The Gastric Sleeve Diet is multifaceted, serving to prepare individuals for surgery, support recuperation, and facilitate a lifelong commitment to healthy eating. This dietary approach is particularly beneficial for those seeking an alternative to surgery or aiming to adopt a healthier lifestyle without the physical alteration of gastric sleeve surgery.

### Gastric Sleeve Diet Phases

The Gastric Sleeve diet comprises four distinct phases, each thoughtfully designed to guide the patient from preparation through recovery and into a sustained, healthy life post-surgery. The success of the Gastric Sleeve diet hinges upon unwavering dedication.

### Phase One: The Initial Week after Surgery

During the first week following surgery, patients are restricted to clear liquids. Adequate hydration is crucial for post-operative healing and minimizes discomfort such as nausea and vomiting. While adhering to a liquid-only regimen might initially prove challenging, those who have undergone surgery often find it relatively manageable due to reduced hunger sensations. Clear liquids should exclude sugary, caffeinated, and carbonated drinks. Opt instead for sugar-free options and maintain a consistent intake of eight glasses of water daily. Permissible clear liquids include broth, sugar-free popsicles, and decaffeinated tea and coffee. This phase prioritizes stomach healing.

### Phase Two: Transition to Protein-Rich Diet

Commencing in the second week post-surgery, patients can gradually transition to a protein-rich, fuller liquid diet. Incorporating sugar-free protein powder facilitates this shift. Consumption of nutrient-dense, non-sugary foods is emphasized, while high-sugar and high-fat options are to be avoided. Protein intake of 20 grams daily is recommended, alongside consistent water consumption. Gradual reintroduction of denser foods, such as mashed potatoes and thinned oatmeal, is possible as the second week concludes. Daily protein intake aims for 60g to 80g by the end of phase two.

### Phase Three: Incorporating Soft Foods

Phase three introduces soft foods with a continued focus on high protein intake (60g to 80g) and hydration. Foods should be sugar-free, and the diet should exclude hard-to-digest items like bread, fatty foods, and raw vegetables. Protein-rich options such as eggs, soft fish, and low-fat cheese are encouraged. Limited caffeine consumption (up to two cups of coffee per day) is permissible.

### Phase Four: Transition to Long-Term Maintenance

Beginning around four weeks post-surgery, phase four marks the transition to a long-term dietary pattern. Those who have not undergone surgery can start at this phase. Protein shakes, providing 60g to 80g of daily protein, remain essential. Hydration continues, while liquids are to be consumed separately from meals. Three small meals and two snacks are advised, emphasizing nutrient-rich, low-sugar, unprocessed foods. Lean meats, vegetables, low-fat cottage cheese, fish, and fruits are suitable choices.

### Recommendations Prior to and Following Bariatric Surgery

*Pre-Surgery (3-4 weeks before):* Adopt a hypocaloric diet supplemented with caloric liquids (vegetable broths, skimmed dairy, infusions) and specific medications like Supradyn or Multi-centrum effervescent and Omeprazole.

*Postoperative Recommendations:*

- Consume 5-6 small, well-chewed meals daily, lasting 20-30 minutes each.
- Separate liquid and solid food intake; avoid exceeding 150 ml of liquid per intake.
- Hydrate with water, sugar-free soft drinks, and infusions; avoid carbonated drinks and alcohol.
- Gradually reintroduce milk, dairy products, and soft foods.
- Avoid simple sugars, fried foods, and low-fiber processed snacks.
- Crushed or liquid-format medications are recommended.
- A bariatric multivitamin may be prescribed.
- Comply with portion control to facilitate stomach adjustment.

### Week One Post-Bariatric Surgery: Liquid Diet

In the initial post-operative week, consume water, sugar-free liquids, and clear liquids like skimmed milk, liquid yogurt, and broths. Aim for at least six daily intakes totaling 2500 ml.

### 15-30 Days Post-Bariatric Surgery: Crushed Diet

Upon reaching this stage, introduce soft, protein-rich foods. Options include scrambled eggs, cooked ham, turkey, low-fat cheeses, and mashed vegetables. Nutritional supplements can be incorporated.

### Example Menu of Mashed Potatoes:

- Zucchini puree, cooked potato, and chicken.
- Mashed carrots, onions, potatoes, and chicken.
- Pureed chard, chickpeas, and cooked egg.
- Pureed broccoli, carrot, rice, and fish.
- Zucchini puree, pasta soup, and lean veal.

By adhering to the Gastric Sleeve diet and its phases, individuals can successfully navigate the journey toward sustained weight loss, optimal health, and a well-adjusted stomach size.

# Chapter 1: Gastric Sleeve Bariatric Surgery and Postoperative Guidelines From 4-8 Weeks

### Introduction: Gastric Sleeve Bariatric Surgery

A normal and healthy diet can be attained through various means, one of which is Gastric Sleeve Bariatric Surgery. This surgical procedure involves the removal of up to 75% of the stomach, leaving behind a slim tube, or "sleeve," capable of accommodating about one ounce of food. By diminishing stomach size, patients experience quicker and shorter-lasting feelings of fullness. Consequently, they consume smaller portions and experience reduced cravings for sugary and high-calorie foods. Notably, Gastric Sleeve Surgery is relatively safe due to its non-invasive nature, and patients have the option to reverse the surgery should their weight trajectory change. This procedure is performed by specialized surgeons, eliminating open incisions and hospital stays. It offers a lasting solution for patients who have struggled with diets and medications without significant success.

### The Gastric Sleeve Procedure and its Benefits

The Gastric Sleeve Procedure effectively eliminates around 70% of the stomach, leaving a slender tube capable of holding approximately one ounce of food. This adjustment replicates a smaller stomach, promoting the intake of reduced amounts per meal. As the body adapts to this change, appetite decreases, and feelings of fullness are

experienced sooner after meals. Smaller, more frequent meals become feasible. While the procedure typically lasts two to three years, patients can potentially undergo a "reverse" gastric sleeve surgery to further modify stomach size if weight changes occur. This dynamic approach empowers individuals to lose weight effectively and sustainably.

### Recommendations Prior to and After Bariatric Surgery

*Weeks Before Bariatric Surgery:* In the preparatory phase, occurring 3-4 weeks prior to surgery, adhering to a HYPOCALORIC DIET (optimal source plus three daily packages) is recommended. Additionally, free intake of caloric liquids, such as vegetable broths, defatted meat, and infusions, is advised. Supplementary medications, like Supradyn or Multi-centrum effervescent (one tablet per day) and Omeprazole 20 mg (one tablet per day), further support the preparation.

*Postoperative Recommendations Bariatric Surgery:* For successful recovery and ongoing health, adhering to the following guidelines is essential:

- Consume 5-6 small meals per day in modest portions, ensuring thorough chewing.
- Allocate 20-30 minutes for each meal.
- Avoid simultaneous consumption of liquids and solid foods; liquids should be consumed approximately 30 minutes before or one hour after meals. Liquid intake per serving should not exceed 150 ml.
- Hydrate with water, sugar-free soft drinks, and infusions. Eschew carbonated and sugary beverages, as well as alcohol.
- Minimize intake of flatulent foods.
- Cease eating before feeling overly full.
- Refrain from ingesting simple sugars (e.g., sugar, honey, jam, chocolate).
- Gradually reintroduce milk and dairy products, initially starting with yogurt and soft cheese. Those with intolerances should avoid these.
- Opt for liquids over solids if fullness occurs prematurely, aiming to prevent gastric discomfort.
- Persistently avoid foods that evoke intolerance, considering retrying them after 3-4 weeks.
- Administer medications in crushed or liquid form.
- Emphasize consumption of foods in non-whole forms.

### Diet After Bariatric Surgery

*First Week: Liquid Diet* During the initial week post-bariatric surgery, focus on liquids, such as water and sugar-free options like infusions. If tolerable, incorporate skimmed milk, liquid yogurt, defatted vegetable/meat broths, and juices without added sugars. Aim for at least six small sips throughout the day, totaling a minimum of 2500 ml. Incorporating Optisource Plus (3 packages daily) in small portions is advised.

In essence, Gastric Sleeve Bariatric Surgery offers an effective path to sustainable weight loss and health improvement. By adhering to postoperative recommendations, patients can successfully navigate their dietary journey, promoting lasting well-being.

# Chapter 2: AT 15-30 DAYS: CRUSHED DIET

**Gastric Sleeve Bariatric Surgery: Phases, Benefits, and Preparation**

**Introduction to Recovery Phases**

Upon entering the 15-30 day recovery phase, patients with good tolerance levels can progressively reintroduce a variety of foods to their diet. This includes scrambled eggs, tortillas soaked in water, cooked ham, turkey, fresh low-fat cheeses, mashed vegetables, crushed carbohydrates, protein sources, fruit porridge or boiled/baked fruit, and skimmed yogurts. It is advisable to continue incorporating Optisource supplements during this period. Additionally, a menu showcasing five types of mashed potatoes is as follows: • Zucchini puree, cooked potato, and cooked chicken. • Mashed carrots, onions, potatoes, and chicken. • Pureed chard, chickpeas, and cooked egg. • Pureed broccoli, carrot, rice, and fish. • Zucchini puree, pasta soup, and lean veal.

**Weeks 4-8: Transition to Normal Diet**

Between weeks 4 to 8, patients can embrace a regular and healthy diet.

**Exploring the Benefits**

While the significance of health is often associated with dietary choices, there's a broader perspective to consider. Weight loss is frequently tied solely to eating habits. Nonetheless, adopting the Vertical Sleeve Gastrectomy offers an alternative approach, facilitating weight loss and additional health enhancements beyond fat reduction. This surgery, performed under sedation and lasting around two hours, can yield significant weight loss along with other notable advantages.

**Advantages of Gastric Sleeve Bariatric Surgery**

**Weight Loss and Health Improvement:** Gastric Sleeve Bariatric Surgery involves a surgeon creating a small incision in the abdomen and reducing stomach capacity. This procedure curbs food intake, potentially leading to a weight loss range of 6-15% at 6 months and 20-30% over two years. Weight loss tends to be sustainable over 3-5 years, with gradual regain. This surgery is particularly beneficial for those with diabetes, metabolic syndrome, a BMI over 50, or limited success with other bariatric procedures. It can reduce overall mortality risk by 40%, as well as risks associated with stroke, diabetes, congestive heart failure, and cancer.

**Safety and Compliance:** Gastric Sleeve Surgery boasts a mortality rate of 0.2%, with a minimal risk of complications like surgical leaks and infection. Post-operative minor interventions may be required. The surgery reduces the risk of hernias by 50% or more and enhances medication compliance. For diabetic patients, the surgery can lead to improved glycemic control by reducing the required insulin levels by 25-

45%. Immediate glycemic control improvements are common. The surgery enables larger food intake without "portion distortion syndrome," often experienced after other procedures.

**Preparing for Surgery and Recovery:**

Understanding the unfamiliar and stressful nature of surgery, here are key steps to manage anxieties before and after the operation:

- Seek support from individuals who have undergone the surgery.
- Attain a clear understanding of the surgical process to reduce fear.
- Balance work and life to manage stress levels effectively.
- Limit caffeine intake to minimize anxiety.
- Consult mental health professionals if necessary.
- Ensure adequate sleep prior to the operation.
- Adhere to pre-operative dietary recommendations and post-operative vitamin intake.
- Utilize painkillers and antibiotics as prescribed.
- Manage smoking habits to facilitate recovery.
- Keep busy to alleviate excessive thoughts about the surgery.
- Limit sugar intake before and after anesthesia.
- Consult a plastic surgery expert for doubts.
- Maintain body temperature during surgery.

**Distinct Phases of Bariatric Surgery**

Bariatric surgery is a significant step for morbidly obese individuals, involving the alteration of the digestive tract to reduce its size. Adequate preparation is crucial before undergoing the procedure. This article provides insights into the phases of recovery and dietary adjustments needed throughout the journey. Starting with understanding gastric sleeve bariatric surgery, patients can expect laparoscopic or open abdominal procedures that modify stomach size to induce early satiety.

**Phase 1: Preparation Phase**

The initial stage of the procedure begins approximately a week after your surgery. During this phase, a feeding tube will be inserted into your stomach via a tube connected to your stomach muscle. Typically, this feeding tube is surgically placed in a vein stemming from either your wrist or hand, based on surgeon preferences. This feeding tube facilitates intravenous fluid and nutrient infusion during this period, along with oral nutritional supplements to compensate for potential food deficiencies during this phase.

Gastric sleeve bariatric surgery is a weight loss surgery type that removes a significant portion, if not all, of the stomach, thereby restricting food intake. If you or someone you know is contemplating this procedure, it's vital to be aware of the dietary guidelines for the preparation phase. Here are some suggestions:

1. **Moderate Portion Sizes:** Opt for smaller portions and distribute your eating throughout the day, avoiding consuming large quantities in one sitting. This approach minimizes the risk of severe gastrointestinal problems. The same principle applies to fluids, as excessive liquid intake right after surgery can lead to diarrhea.

2. **Limit Stimulants:** Refrain from stimulants like caffeine, recreational drugs, alcohol, cigarettes, and food additives.

3. **Low-Fat Foods:** Steer clear of foods rich in fats.

4. **Prioritize Protein:** Include protein-rich foods such as meat, poultry, fish, cheese, soy products, and egg whites. These support stable blood sugar levels.

5. **Stress Management:** Minimize stress during the preparation phase. Reducing stress helps in detoxifying the body and preventing potential illness due to accumulated toxins.

6. **Wound Healing Foods:** Avoid foods that hinder wound healing, such as hard cheese, cooked or raw shellfish, and high-sugar items.

7. **Limit Saturated Fats:** Stay away from saturated fats present in meats and butter.

8. **Avoid High-Fat Dairy:** Steer clear of high-fat dairy products like butterfat-rich items, ice cream, and mayonnaise. These can lead to increased abdominal fat due to the release of substances like butyrate, inducing inflammation.

9. **Water Retention Foods:** Prevent water retention by avoiding foods containing saponins, like green beans, beets, soybeans, and cauliflower.

10. **Avoid Heavy Foods:** Cut out heavy foods like fatty meats, bacon, and certain fish, as these can apply pressure to the stomach vessels, potentially leading to bleeding during healing.

11. **Eliminate Sugar:** Absolutely avoid sugar, even if it's concealed in natural products like fruit juice. Check labels for added sugar.

12. **Steer Clear of Carbonated Beverages:** Carbonated drinks can cause gas in the stomach.

### Phase 2: Transition Phase

In this stage, incisions and inserted tubes will have healed. However, you'll still have a feeding tube through your wrist or hand, which you'll use for adequate water intake and IV fluids. Protein drinks and supplements will help kickstart metabolism, considering that gastric sleeve surgery alters stomach size and absorption capacity. Here's guidance for the transition phase:

- Begin with softer foods like soups and mashed potatoes on your first day back home.

- Stick to clear liquids initially, moving to pureed foods after 48 hours. Avoid carbonated and caffeinated beverages.

- Opt for soft foods during the first few days, with protein shakes being an exception.

- Fat aids swallowing and digestion. Choose sources like butter, oil, and cream, but don't overdo it.

- Maintain small portions and intervals (6-8 hours) between meals.

- Eating in smaller quantities prevents nausea, pain, and overeating. 200-400 calories per meal is ideal.

- Steer clear of high-fat, high-sugar, and high-salt foods.

- Avoid solid foods close to pain medication intake.

- Skip high-fiber and heavy foods before bedtime.

- Stop eating when full, and avoid overeating to prevent nausea and vomiting.

- Don't eat before sleeping.

- Drink water and diluted fruit juices. Avoid tea, coffee, and sodas.

## Phase 3: Recovery Phase

Following removal of tubes and stitches, return to normal eating habits. Bariatric surgery patients often consume 4-6 meals per day, each containing 2-3 ounces of lean protein, vegetables, and whole grains. You might need a vitamin and mineral supplement to counter nutrient deficiencies caused by the surgery's restrictive nature.

## Additional Advice for Successful Recovery:

- Mentally prepare for surgery by understanding the process.

- Manage anxiety and stress before surgery.

- Maintain a balanced lifestyle to control anxiety.

- Get adequate sleep for recovery.

- Follow pre-operative instructions, including diet and vitamins.

- Don't forget prescribed painkillers and antibiotics.

- Minimize caffeine and tobacco intake.

- Think positively and focus on recovery.

- Communicate your fears with someone trustworthy.

- Stay hydrated and warm during surgery.

- Stick to postoperative care instructions and consult a doctor if problems arise.

**Benefits of Vertical Sleeve Gastrectomy (VSG):**

- Substantial weight loss compared to other surgeries.

- Reduces risk of type 2 diabetes and obesity-related issues.

- No malabsorption or vitamin deficiency.

- Avoids dumping syndrome and reflux.

- Consider potential reversibility.

**Eating at Restaurants with VSG:**

- Order appetizers instead of full courses.

- Carry a water bottle to control hunger.

- Avoid excessive bread intake.

- Have a backup set of sleeves.

- Opt for smaller portions.

- Choose low-calorie dressings and sauces.

- Eat slowly and savor the experience.

- Stay mindful and avoid overeating.

- Skip desserts or opt for lighter options.

- Embrace new foods and preparations.

Remember, the journey to recovery requires diligence and consistency. By adhering to these guidelines, you'll enhance your chances of a successful post-operative period and reap the benefits of the surgery. Always consult with your medical professional before making any decisions related to your recovery process.

# CHAPTER 3 CLEAR FLUIDS (LIQUID DIET)

## 1. PEPPERMINT TEA

Preparation Time: 1 minute

Cooking Time: 5 minutes

Servings: 2-3

**INGREDIENTS:**

- Hot water (4 c)
- Peppermint leaf, dried (.5 c.)

**DIRECTIONS:**

1. Set your water to a boil. Once it starts to boil, add in the peppermint leaves and then take it all off the heat.
2. Cover the pot and allow it to cool for a few minutes.
3. When it is cooled down, strain out the mixture and serve.

**NUTRITION:**Calories 34.2 Carbs 9.1g Fat 0g Protein 0.1g

## ALMOND TEA

Preparation Time: 1 minute

Cooking Time: 5 minutes

Servings: 2-3

**INGREDIENTS:**

- Water (1 c.)
- Cinnamon (1 tsp.)
- Almond powder (5 Tbsp.)

**DIRECTIONS:**

1. Bring out a pan and place it on some high heat. Add in the water with the rest of the ingredients.
2. Bring it to boil and when boiling, take it off the heat.
3. Serve warm and enjoy.

**NUTRITION:**Calories 40 Carbs 1.4g Fat 3g Protein 1.5g

## ORANGE VANILLA TEA

Preparation Time: 2 minutes

Cooking Time: 8 minutes

Servings: 2-3

**INGREDIENTS:**

- Vanilla (.25 tsp.)
- Sliced oranges (2)
- Water (.25 c.)

**DIRECTIONS:**

1. Take out a pan and add it to high heat on the stove. Add in the ingredients and then allow this to boil.
2. Take the pan off the heat and give it time to sit for a few minutes.
3. When the mixture is cooled down, strain it out before serving.

**NUTRITION:** Calories 60 Carbs 14g Fat 1g Protein 2g

---

## KIWI SORBET

Preparation Time: 5 minutes

Cooking Time: 5 minutes

Servings: 2-3

**INGREDIENTS:**

- Grated orange zest (1 Tbsp.)
- Chopped kiwi fruit (.5 lb.)
- Crushed ice cubes (4.5 c.)

**DIRECTIONS:**

1. Add all of the ingredients above into a blender.
2. Blend them together for half a minute and then serve and enjoy.

**NUTRITION:** Calories 105 Carbs 26g Fat 0.3g Protein 0.6g

---

## ALCOHOL-FREE MINT MOJITO

Preparation Time: 20 minutes

Cooking Time: 5 minutes

Servings: 2-3

**INGREDIENTS:**

- Water (2 c.)
- Natural sweetener (.5 c.)
- Lime juice (1 oz.)
- Mint leaves (.5 c)

**DIRECTIONS:**

1. Add the sweetener and water to a pot and give it time to boil so the syrup can thicken.
2. Move the mint leaves to a jar and add in the syrup. Cover it up and allow this to steep for a bit.
3. After 20 minutes, you can create a mixture of one tablespoon of the syrup and half a cup of water along with the lime juice. Mix and enjoy.

**NUTRITION:** Calories 32 Carbs 3g Fat 0g Protein 0g

---

## APRICOT AND ORANGE JUICE

Preparation Time: 10 minutes

Cooking Time: 0 minutes

Servings: 2-3

**INGREDIENTS:**

- Peeled ginger slice (1)
- Peeled lemon (1)
- Green grapes (1 c.)
- Pomegranate seeds (1 c.)
- Pitted apricots (2)
- Peeled oranges (2)

**DIRECTIONS:**

1. Peel up the oranges and then divide all of them into wedges before setting aside.
2. Wash off the apricots and slice in half. Take the pits out and slice into smaller pieces.

3. Cut the tops of the pomegranate fruit with a sharp knife and then slice down the white membrane that is found in both.
4. Pop the seeds into a measuring cup and then set it to the side.
5. Peel the lemon and cut it lengthwise in half and put it to the side.

6. Peel the slices of ginger and add to the side as well.
7. In a juicer add the ginger, lemon, pomegranate, apricots, and oranges into it. Process until well juiced and then chill a few minutes before serving.

**NUTRITION:**Calories 196 Carbs 48g Fat 0.8g Protein 4g

## CHICKEN BONE BROTH

Preparation Time: 5 minutes

Cooking Time: 2 hours

Servings: 2-3

### INGREDIENTS:

- 1 oz. chicken bones, cleaned
- 2 tablespoons apple cider vinegar
- 1 onion, sliced
- 5-6 garlic cloves
- 1 tablespoon cooking oil
- ½ teaspoon salt
- ½ teaspoon white pepper

- 1-inch ginger slice
- 6 cups water

### DIRECTIONS:

1. In a large skillet add chicken bones with water, onion, garlic, ginger, oil, vinegar, salt, pepper, and stir. Cover with lid.
2. Leave to cook on low heat for 2 hours.
3. Strain the broth and discard residue.
4. Serve hot and enjoy.

**NUTRITION:**Calories 147 Total Fat 5 g Carbohydrate 9 g Protein 10 g

## LEMON, MINT & CUCUMBER INFUSED WATER

Preparation Time: 5 minutes + 2 hours chilling time

Cooking Time: 0 minutes

Servings: 2-3

### INGREDIENTS:

- 6 cups water
- 1 grapefruit, sliced
- 1 orange, sliced

- ½ cup cucumber slices

### DIRECTIONS:

1. Combine all the ingredients in a pitcher.
2. Refrigerate for 2 hours or overnight.
3. Serve in the morning and/or drink through the day.

**NUTRITION:**Calories 1.3 Total Fat 0.0 g Carbohydrate 0.4 g Protein 0.0 g

## CITRUS & MINT INFUSED WATER

Preparation Time: 5 minutes + 2 hours chilling time

Cooking Time: 0 minutes

Servings: 2-3

### INGREDIENTS:

- ½ red grapefruit, segmented
- 2 mint leaves
- ½ lemon, sliced

- 1 cucumber, sliced
- ½ lime sliced
- ½ gallon spring water

### DIRECTIONS:

1. Wash and prepare the ingredients.
2. Place all the ingredients in a pitcher.
3. Refrigerate for 2 hours.
4. Serve after.

**NUTRITION:**Calories 2 Total Fat 0.0 g Carbohydrate 0.4 g Protein 0.0 g

## PINEAPPLE AND MANGO WATER

Preparation Time: 5 minutes + 1 hour chilling time

Cooking Time: 0 minutes

Servings: 2-3

**INGREDIENTS:**

- 1 cup pineapple slices
- 1 cup ripe mango, chunks
- 10 cups water
- ½ teaspoon protein powder
- 1-inch ginger sliced, peeled

**DIRECTIONS:**

1. Transfer all ingredients into a pitcher and place to chill for at least an hour.
2. Pour into serving glasses and serve.

**NUTRITION:**Calories 10 Total Fat 0.0 g Carbohydrate 12 g Protein 0.0 g

## HONEYDEW & KIWI INFUSED WATER

Preparation Time: 5 minutes + 1 hour chilling time

Cooking Time: 0 minutes

Servings: 2-3

**INGREDIENTS:**

- 1 kiwi, peeled and sliced
- 2 cups honeydew melon, chopped
- 10 cups Water

**DIRECTIONS:**

1. In a pitcher combine the fruits.
2. Fill to the top with water.
3. Refrigerate for 1 hour before serving.

**NUTRITION:**Calories 12 Total Fat 0.0 g Carbohydrate 4.4 g Protein 0.0 g

## SWEET AND SOUR LYCHEE INFUSED WATER

Preparation Time: 5 minutes + 1 hour chilling time

Cooking Time: 0 minutes

Servings: 2-3

**INGREDIENTS:**

- 1 cup lychees, peeled, seeded
- 1 tbsp. ginger powder
- 10 cups water
- 3 tablespoons lemon juice

**DIRECTIONS:**

1. Combine all your ingredients in a pitcher.
2. Refrigerate for 1 hour before serving.

**NUTRITION:** Calories 2 Total Fat 0.0 g Carbohydrate 31g Protein 0.0 g

## KIWI AND KALE DETOX WATER

Preparation Time: 5 minutes + 1 hour chilling time

Cooking Time: 0 minutes

Servings: 2-3

**INGREDIENTS:**

- 4 kiwis, sliced
- 5 kale leaves
- 10 cups cold water

**DIRECTIONS:**

1. Combine all your ingredients in a pitcher.
2. Refrigerate for 1 hour before serving.

**NUTRITION:**Calories 1.7 Total Fat 0.0g Carbohydrate 8 g Protein 17 g

## WATERMELON AND LEMON WATER

Preparation Time: 10 minutes

Cooking Time: 0 minutes

Servings: 2-3

### INGREDIENTS:

- 3 cups watermelon, chunks, seeded
- 3 tablespoons lemon juice
- 2-3 mint leaves
- 1 pinch salt
- 10 cups water

### DIRECTIONS:

1. Combine all your ingredients in a pitcher.
2. Refrigerate for 1 hour before serving.

NUTRITION:Calories 105.1 Total Fat 1.4 g Carbohydrate 24.6 g Protein 2.1 g

## MANGO & GINGER INFUSED WATER

Preparation Time: 5 minutes + 3 hours chilling time

Cooking Time: 0 minutes

Servings: 2-3

### INGREDIENTS:

- 1 cup diced mango
- 1-inch ginger, peeled and sliced
- 2 cups ice
- Water, to top off

### DIRECTIONS:

1. Peel and slice the ginger in 3-4 coin size slices.
2. Transfer the ginger into a pitcher along with mango.
3. Top with 2 cups ice and fill with water.
4. Refrigerate for 3 hours.
5. Serve.

NUTRITION:Calories 1.3 Total Fat 0.0 g Carbohydrate 0.4 g Protein 0.0 g

## LAVENDER & BLUEBERRY INFUSED WATER

Preparation Time: 5 minutes + 1 hour chilling time

Cooking Time: 0 minutes

Servings: 2-3

### INGREDIENTS:

- 8 cups water
- 1-pint fresh blueberries
- 1 tablespoon lavender flowers

### DIRECTIONS:

1. Mix all your ingredients in a large pitcher.
2. Stir gently and refrigerate for 1 hour.
3. Strain and serve with ice.

NUTRITION:Calories 1.3 Total Fat 0.0 g Carbohydrate 0.4 g Protein 0.0 g

## PINA COLADA INFUSED WATER

Preparation Time: 5 minutes + chilling time

Cooking Time: 0 minutes

Servings: 2-3

### INGREDIENTS:

- 1 cup peeled and thinly sliced pineapple
- 2 cups ice
- 6 cups Coconut Water

### DIRECTIONS:

1. Pour out your pineapple into a large pitcher.
2. Top with ice.
3. Pour in water to the top and cover.
4. Refrigerate for 1 hour before serving.

**NUTRITION:** Calories 1.3 Total Fat 0.0 g Carbohydrate 0.4 g Protein 0.0 g

## ORANGE, STRAWBERRY & MINT INFUSED WATER

Preparation Time: 5 minutes + chilling time

Cooking Time: 0 minutes

Servings: 2-3

### INGREDIENTS:

- 2 oranges, cut into wedges
- ½ cup strawberries
- 4 leaves mint
- 6 cups water

### DIRECTIONS:

1. Place all the ingredients into a pitcher.
2. Cover and allow to chill for a minimum of 2 hours or overnight.
3. Serve.

**NUTRITION:** Calories 1.3 Total Fat 0.0 g Carbohydrate 0.4 g Protein 0.0 g

## WATERMELON JUICE

Preparation Time: 5 minutes;

Cooking Time: 0 minutes;

Serving: 2

### INGREDIENTS

- 1 watermelon, peeled, deseeded, cubed
- 1 tablespoon date sugar
- ½ of key lime, juiced, zest
- 2 cups soft-jelly coconut water

### DIRECTIONS

1. Place watermelon pieces in a high-speed food processor or blender, add lime zest and juice, add date sugar and then pulse until smooth.
2. Take two tall glasses, fill them with watermelon mixture until two-third full, and then pour in coconut water.
3. Stir until mixed and then serve.
4. Storage instructions:
5. Divide drink between two jars or bottles, cover with a lid and then store the containers in the refrigerator for up to 3 days.

**NUTRITION:** 55 Calories; 1.3 g Fats; 0.9 g Protein; 9.9 g Carbohydrates; 7 g Fiber;

## GINGER TEA

Preparation Time: 5 minutes

Cooking Time: 5 minutes

Servings: 2-3

### INGREDIENTS:

- Boiling water (3 c.)
- Grated ginger root (3 tsp.)

### DIRECTIONS:

1. Combine all of the ingredients together before allowing them to sit and rest for ten minutes or so. 2.Serve and enjoy.

**NUTRITION:** Calories 1.3 Total Fat 0.0 g Carbohydrate 0.4 g Protein 0.0 g

## ORANGE JUICE

Preparation Time: 10 minutes

Cooking Time: 5 minutes

Servings: 2-3

### INGREDIENTS:

- 6 medium oranges; peeled, seeded, and pieced

### DIRECTIONS:

1. In a juicer, add orange pieces and extract the juice according to manufacturer's directions.

2. Transfer into two glasses and serve immediately.

**NUTRITION:** Calories 259 Fats 0.1 g Cholesterol 0 mg Carbohydrates 64.9 g Fiber 13.3 g Protein 5.3g

## KEY LIME TEA

Preparation Time: 5 minutes;

Cooking Time: 5 minutes;

Servings: 2-3

### INGREDIENTS:

- 1 sprig of dill weed
- 1/16 teaspoon cayenne pepper
- 1 tablespoon key lime juice
- 2 cups spring water

### DIRECTIONS:

1. Take a medium saucepan, place it over medium-high heat, pour in water, and then bring it to a boil.
2. Boil for 5 minutes, and then strain the tea into a bowl.
3. Add lime juice stir until mixed and then stir in cayenne pepper.
4. Divide tea between two mugs and then serve.

**NUTRITION:** 2.4 Calories; 0 g Fats; 0 g Protein; 0.5 g Carbohydrates; 0 g Fiber

## STRAWBERRY JUICE

Preparation Time: 10 minutes

Cooking Time: 5 minutes

Servings: 2-3

### INGREDIENTS:

- 2 cups fresh strawberries, hulled
- 1 teaspoon fresh key lime juice
- 2 cups chilled spring water

### DIRECTIONS:

1. In a high-powered blender, put all Ingredients: and pulse well.
2. Through a strainer, strain the juice and transfer into 2 glasses.
3. Serve immediately.

**NUTRITION:** Calories 46 Fats 0 g Cholesterol 0 mg Carbohydrates 11.1 g Fiber 2.9 g Protein 1 g

## GRAPE JUICE

Preparation Time: 10 minutes

Cooking Time: 5 minutes

Servings: 2-3

### INGREDIENTS:

- 2 cups seedless red grapes
- ½ lime
- 2 cups spring water

### DIRECTIONS:

1. In a blender, put all Ingredients: and pulse well.
2. Through a strainer, strain the juice and transfer into 2 glasses.
3. Serve immediately.

**NUTRITION:** Calories 63 Fats 0.1 g Cholesterol 0 mg Carbohydrates 16.2 g Fiber 0.9 g Protein 0.6

## MANGO JUICE

Preparation Time: 10 minutes

Cooking Time: 5 minutes

Servings: 2-3

### INGREDIENTS:

- 4 cups mangoes; peeled, pitted, and chopped
- 2 cups spring water

**DIRECTIONS:**

1. In a blender, put all Ingredients: and pulse well.
2. Through a strainer, strain the juice and transfer into 4 glasses.
3. Serve immediately.

**NUTRITION:** Calories 99 Fats 0.2 g Cholesterol 0 mg Carbohydrates 24.7 g Fiber 2.6 g Protein 1.4 g

---

## APPLE & KALE JUICE

Preparation Time: 10 minutes

Cooking Time: 5 minutes

Servings: 2-3

**INGREDIENTS:**

- 2 large green apples, cored and sliced
- 4 cups fresh kale leaves
- ¼ cup fresh parsley leaves
- 1 tablespoon fresh ginger, peeled
- 1 key lime, peeled and seeded
- 1 cup chilled spring water

**DIRECTIONS:**

1. In a blender, put all Ingredients: and pulse well.
2. Through a strainer, strain the juice and transfer into 2 glasses.
3. Serve immediately

**NUTRITION:** Calories 196 Fats 0.1 g Cholesterol 0 mg Carbohydrates 47.9 g Fiber 8.2 g Protein 5.2 g

---

## WATERMELON AND STRAWBERRIES DRINK

Preparation Time: 5 minutes;

Cooking Time: 0 minutes;

Servings: 2-3

**INGREDIENTS:**

- 1 cup strawberries
- 1 cup watermelon, chunks
- 1 tsp date
- 1 cup soft jelly coconut water

**DIRECTIONS:**

1. Plug in a high-speed food processor or blender and add all the Ingredients: in its jar.
2. Cover the blender jar with its lid and then pulse for 40 to 60 seconds until smooth.
3. Divide the drink between two glasses and then serve.

**NUTRITION:** 110 Calories; 0 g Fats; 0 g Protein; 28 g Carbohydrates; 6 g Fiber;

---

## CLEAR VEGETABLE STOCK

Preparation time: 10 min

Cooking time: 15 min

Servings: 4-5

**INGREDIENTS:**

- 1 tbsp. olive oil
- 1 onion
- 1 stalks of celery
- 1 carrots
- 1 bunch chopped green onions
- 2 minced cloves garlic
- 2 sprigs parsley, fresh
- 2 sprigs thyme, fresh
- 2 bay leaves
- 1 tsp. salt
- 2 quarts water

**DIRECTIONS:**

1. Chop scrubbed vegetables into 1-inch chunks.
2. Heat oil in a soup pot. Add onion, celery, carrots, green onions, bay leaves, thyme, parsley, and garlic. Cook over high heat 5-10 minutes, stirring frequently.
3. Add salt and water and bring to a boil. Simmer for 30 minutes on low.

# CHAPTER 4 FULL LIQUIDS (PUREE DIET)

## 1. PIÑA COLADA SMOOTHIE

Preparation Time: 10 minutes

Cooking Time: 8 minutes to chill

Servings: 2-3

INGREDIENTS:

- ½ cup canned pineapple chunks, drained
- 4 ounces unsweetened coconut milk
- ½ cup nonfat plain Greek yogurt
- ½ teaspoon coconut extract

DIRECTIONS:

1. With a blender, combine the pineapple, coconut milk, yogurt, and coconut extract.
2. Blend until smooth, or until your desired consistency is reached. Pour into a glass and enjoy.
3. Alternatively, refrigerate for 10 to 15 minutes to chill before sipping.

NUTRITION: Protein: 13g; Calories: 148; Fat: 3g; Carbohydrates: 19g; Fiber: 1g; Total sugar: 17g; Added sugar: 0g; Sodium: 46mg

## GREEN MANGO SMOOTHIE

Preparation Time: 10 minutes

Cooking Time: 2 minutes

Servings: 2-3

INGREDIENTS:

- ⅓ avocado, peeled and pitted
- ⅓ cup fresh spinach
- ½ cup canned mango chunks, drained
- ½ cup nonfat plain Greek yogurt
- ½ cup nonfat milk
- 1 teaspoon honey or sugar-free vanilla syrup

DIRECTIONS:

1. In a blender, combine the avocado, spinach, mango, yogurt, milk, and honey.
2. Blend until smooth, or until your desired consistency is reached. Pour into a glass and enjoy.

NUTRITION: Protein: 21g; Calories: 261; Fat: 8g; Carbohydrates: 30g; Fiber: 5g; Total sugar: 24g; Added sugar: 6g; Sodium: 117mg

## PEACHY GREEK YOGURT PANNA COTTA

Preparation Time: 10 minutes

Cooking Time: 5 minutes & 2-8 hours to chill

Servings: 2-3

**INGREDIENTS:**

- ½ cup nonfat milk
- 1½ tablespoons honey
- 1 tablespoon unflavored powdered gelatin
- 1½ cups nonfat plain Greek yogurt
- ½ teaspoon vanilla extract (optional)
- ½ cup canned no-sugar-added sliced peaches, drained

1. In a small saucepan over low heat, heat the milk for 2 to 4 minutes until lukewarm. Add the honey and gelatin. Cook for 3 to 5 minutes, stirring, until the honey and gelatin dissolve. (Do not bring to a boil.) Remove from the heat.
2. In a small bowl, whisk the yogurt until smooth. Add the warm gelatin mixture and vanilla (if using). Whisk well to combine. Pour into 4 small jars, glasses, or ramekins. Refrigerate for at least 2 hours or overnight for best results.
3. Before serving, put the canned peaches into a blender or food processor and puree until smooth.
4. Top each panna cotta with 2 tablespoons of pureed peach and enjoy.

**NUTRITION:** Protein: 12g; Calories: 106; Fat: 1g; Carbohydrates: 13g; Fiber: <1g; Total sugar: 13g; Added sugar: 7g; Sodium: 48mg

**DIRECTIONS:**

## NUTTY CREAMY WHEAT BOWL

Preparation Time: 5 minutes

Cooking Time: 5 minutes

Servings: 2-3

**INGREDIENTS:**

- 4 ounces nonfat milk
- 1 tablespoon uncooked Cream of Wheat
- Salt
- 1 teaspoon almond butter
- Ground cinnamon, for seasoning
- ½ banana, mashed

**DIRECTIONS:**

1. In a small saucepan or pot, stir together the milk and Cream of Wheat until combined. Place the pot over medium-high heat and bring the mixture to a boil, whisking frequently to keep lumps from forming.
2. Reduce the heat to low and simmer the cereal for 1 to 2 minutes, just until it thickens. Season with salt to taste and pour the cereal into a bowl.
3. Add the almond butter and season with cinnamon. Top the cereal with mashed banana before enjoying.

**NUTRITION:** Protein: 10; Calories: 167; Fat: 3g; Carbohydrates: 26g; Fiber: 2g; Total sugar: 11g; Added sugar: 0g; Sodium: 127mg

## BAKED CINNAMON-APPLE RICOTTA

Preparation Time: 10 minutes

Cooking Time: 8 minutes

Servings: 2-3

**INGREDIENTS:**

- ½ cup part-skim ricotta
- ¼ cup no-sugar-added applesauce

- 1 teaspoon ground cinnamon
- Ground nutmeg, for seasoning (optional)

**DIRECTIONS:**

1. Preheat the oven to 375°F.
2. Spoon the ricotta into a 6-ounce ramekin. Top with the applesauce and sprinkle with the cinnamon and nutmeg (if using) to taste.
3. Bake for 15 minutes, or until hot. Remove and let cool slightly before enjoying warm.

**NUTRITION:** 14g; Calories: 202; Fat: 10g; Carbohydrates: 15g; Fiber: 2g; Total sugar: 6g; Added sugar: 0g; Sodium: 123mg

## DECADENT TOMATO-BASIL SOUP

Preparation Time: 10 minutes

Cooking Time: 10 minutes

Servings: 2-3

**INGREDIENTS:**

- 2 tablespoons olive oil
- ¼ cup diced purple onion
- 1 (15-ounce) can low-sodium whole tomatoes or diced tomatoes, with their juices
- 8 ounces low-sodium chicken broth or vegetable broth
- 1 teaspoon dried basil
- 2 teaspoons honey
- 1 teaspoon aged balsamic vinegar (optional)
- Salt
- Freshly ground black pepper
- 8 tablespoons nonfat plain Greek yogurt

**DIRECTIONS:**

1. In a medium saucepan over medium heat, heat the oil. Add the onion and sauté for about 5 minutes until golden.
2. Stir in the tomatoes with their juices, chicken broth, and basil and bring the soup to a boil. Reduce the heat to low, cover the pan, and simmer the soup for 10 to 15 minutes. Remove from the heat.
3. Carefully pour the soup into a blender and blend on high speed until smooth. Add the honey and vinegar (if using). Season with salt and pepper to taste. Pour into glasses or bowls. Top each serving with 2 tablespoons of yogurt for extra protein and enjoy.

**NUTRITION:** Protein: 4g; Calories: 121; Fat: 7g; Carbohydrates: 9g; Fiber: 1g; Total sugar: 7g; Added sugar: 3g; Sodium: 164mg

## EASY GREEN PEA AND HAM SOUP

Preparation Time: 10 minutes

Cooking Time: 10 minutes

Servings: 2-3

**INGREDIENTS:**

- 1 tablespoon olive oil
- 1 (10-ounce) package frozen peas
- 4 ounces ham, cut into ¼-inch cubes
- 1½ cups low-sodium chicken broth or vegetable broth
- ⅓ cup nonfat plain Greek yogurt
- Freshly ground black pepper
- Chopped fresh parsley, for garnish

**DIRECTIONS:**

1. In a medium saucepan over medium-high heat, heat the oil.

2. Add the peas, ham, and chicken broth and bring to a boil. Cook for about 10 minutes, or until the peas are very soft. Remove from the heat.
3. Carefully pour the soup into a blender and puree until smooth. Pour into bowls or cups. Top each serving with 1 tablespoon of yogurt and season with pepper to taste. Garnish with parsley and enjoy.

**NUTRITION:** Protein: 11g; Calories: 116; Fat: 4g; Carbohydrates: 9g; Fiber: 3g; Total sugar: 4g; Added sugar: 0g; Sodium: 327mg

## CLAM CHOWDER

Preparation Time: 10 minutes

Cooking Time: 5 minutes

Servings: 2-3

### INGREDIENTS:

- ½ onion, chopped
- 1 carrot, diced
- 1 stalk celery, diced
- 1 clove garlic, minced
- ½ tablespoon Creole seasoning
- Sea salt and ground black pepper, to taste
- 1 cup seafood stock
- 1 ripe tomato, puréed
- 1 tablespoon tomato paste
- 1 bay leaf
- ½ pound (227 g) clams, chopped
- 1 tablespoon flaxseed meal

### DIRECTIONS:

1. Heat a pan.
2. Now, sauté the onion, carrot, celery, and garlic
3. Add the remaining ingredients, except for the chopped clams, to the pan.
4. Add the lid and cook for 4 minutes at High heat. Once cooking is complete, carefully remove the lid.
5. Stir in the chopped clams and flaxseed meal.
6. Let it simmer for 2 to 3 minutes longer at medium heat or until everything is heated through.
7. Serve in individual bowls topped with the reserved bacon. Bon appétit!

**NUTRITION:** calories: 264 | fat: 9.4g | protein: 20.8g | carbs: 26.2g | net carbs: 20.2g | fiber: 6.0g

## POTATO MASH

Preparation Time: 5 minutes

Cooking Time: 8 minutes

Servings: 2-3

### INGREDIENTS:

- 2 cups peeled, diced russet potatoes (2½ medium potatoes)
- 1 cup part-skim shredded Cheddar cheese
- 1 cup nonfat plain Greek yogurt

### DIRECTIONS:

1. Fill the bottom of a medium saucepan with a couple inches of water and insert a steamer basket. Place the potatoes in the steamer basket, bring the water to a boil, cover, and steam for about 15 minutes, until softened. Remove from the heat.
2. Add the potatoes, Cheddar cheese, and yogurt to a blender or food processor. Blend the mixture on low for about 2 minutes or until smooth. Enjoy.

**NUTRITION:** calories: 144 | fat: 7.0g | protein: 11.0g | carbs: 10.0g | net carbs: 9.0g | fiber: 1.0g

## SHRIMP AND PARSNIP BISQUE

Preparation Time: 10 minutes

Cooking Time: 5 minutes

Servings: 2-3

### INGREDIENTS:

- 1 tablespoon butter
- ⅓ cup white onion, chopped
- ½ celery rib, chopped
- 1 parsnip, chopped
- ½ carrot, chopped
- 1 tablespoon all-purpose flour
- ¼ cup sherry wine
- Sea salt and ground black pepper
- ½ cup tomato purée
- 1½ cups chicken bone broth
- 8 ounces (227 g) shrimp, deveined
- ½ cup heavy whipping cream

**DIRECTIONS:**

1. In a pan melt the butter. Once hot, add the onion, celery, parsnip, and carrot until softened.
2. Add the flour and cook for 3 minutes more or until everything is well coated. Pour in sherry wine to deglaze the pot.
3. Now, add the salt, pepper, tomato purée, and broth.
4. Place the lid and cook for 5 minutes at high heat. Once cooking is complete carefully remove the lid.
5. Now, add the shrimp and heavy cream and cook on the medium heat for a further 2 to 3 minutes or until everything is heated through. Bon appétit!

**NUTRITION:**362 | fat: 18.9g | protein: 29.6g | carbs: 20.3g | net carbs: 17.5g | fiber: 2.8g

## SALMON CURRY

Preparation Time: 10 minutes

Cooking Time: 5 minutes

Servings: 2-3

### INGREDIENTS:

- 1 tablespoon butter
- 3 curry leaves
- ½ onion, chopped
- 1 clove garlic, crushed
- 1 (1-inch) piece fresh ginger, grated
- ½ dried Kashmiri chili, minced
- ½ cup canned tomatoes, crushed
- ½ teaspoon turmeric powder
- ½ teaspoon ground coriander
- ½ teaspoon ground cumin
- kosher salt and ground black pepper, to taste
- 5 ounces (142 g) can coconut milk
- ¾ pound (340 g) salmon fillets
- 1 tablespoon lemon juice

**DIRECTIONS:**

1. In a pan melt the butter. Once hot, cook the curry leaves for about 30 seconds.
2. Stir in the onions, garlic, ginger and Kashmiri chili and cook for 2 minutes more or until they are fragrant.
3. Add the tomatoes, turmeric, coriander, cumin, salt, and black pepper. Continue to sauté for 30 seconds more.
4. Add the coconut milk and salmon.
5. Place the lid and cook for 2 minutes at Low heat. Once cooking is complete, remove the lid.
6. Spoon the fish curry into individual bowls. Drizzle lemon juice over the fish curry and serve. Enjoy!

**NUTRITION:**calories: 363 | fat: 18.8g | protein: 35.1g | carbs: 10.5g | net carbs: 8.2g | fiber: 2.3g

## COCONUT AND CORNMEAL PORRIDGE

Preparation Time: 15 minutes

Cooking Time: 6 minutes

Servings: 2-3

### INGREDIENTS:

- 6 cups water
- 1¼ cups coconut milk
- 1¼ cups yellow cornmeal, fine
- 2½ sticks cinnamon
- 1¼ teaspoons vanilla extract

- ¾ teaspoon coconut flakes
- ¾ cup sweetened condensed milk

**DIRECTIONS:**

1. Add 5 cups of water and all the coconut milk to a pan.
2. Mix the cornmeal with 1 cup of water and add the mixture to the pot.
3. Stir in vanilla extract, coconut flakes, and cinnamon sticks.
4. Place the lid.
5. Cook for 6 minutes at high heat stirring occasionally.
6. Remove the lid.
7. Stir in sweetened condensed milk.
8. Serve and enjoy.

**NUTRITION:** calories: 253 | fat: 3.1g | protein: 6.9g | carbs: 46.2g | net carbs: 46.2g | fiber: 0g

## COCONUT AND RICE PUDDING

Preparation Time: 5 minutes

Cooking Time: 5 minutes

Servings: 2-3

**INGREDIENTS:**

- 1 cup coconut milk
- ¾ cup water
- ½ cup basmati rice, short grain
- ½ cup coconut cream
- 2 tablespoons maple syrup
- A pinch of sea salt
- Whipped cream and coconut flakes for garnishing

**DIRECTIONS:**

1. Add all the listed ingredients except for the whipped cream, and coconut flakes to a pan.
2. Place the lid.
3. Cook for 15 minutes at medium heat, stirring occasionally.
4. Remove the lid.
5. Stir the prepared pudding and serve in a bowl.
6. Add the whipped cream and coconut flakes on top.

**NUTRITION:** calories: 476 | fat: 27.9g | protein: 18.6g | carbs: 36.5g | net carbs: 35.1g | fiber: 1.4g

## PIMENTO BERRY AND CORNMEAL PORRIDGE

Preparation Time: 10 minutes

Cooking Time: 6 minutes

Servings: 2-3

**INGREDIENTS:**

- 6 cups water
- 1¼ cups milk
- 1¼ cups yellow cornmeal, fine
- 2½ sticks cinnamon
- 5 pimento berries
- 1¼ teaspoons vanilla extract
- ¾ teaspoon nutmeg, ground
- ¾ cup sweetened condensed milk

**DIRECTIONS:**

1. Add 5 cups of water and the milk to the Instant Pot.
2. Mix the cornmeal with 1 cup of water and add it to the pot.
3. Stir in vanilla extract, pimento berries, nutmeg, and cinnamon sticks.
4. Secure the lid of the cooker and press the Manual function key.
5. Adjust the time to 6 minutes and cook at high pressure.
6. After the beep, release the pressure naturally and remove the lid.
7. Stir in sweetened condensed milk.
8. Serve and enjoy.

**NUTRITION:** calories: 247 | fat: 5.4g | protein: 6.9g | carbs: 43.5g | net carbs: 40.5g | fiber: 3.0g

## BROWN RICE AND RAISIN PUDDING

Preparation Time: 5 minutes

Cooking Time: 15 minutes

Servings: 2-3

### INGREDIENTS:

- 1 cup short grain brown rice
- 1½ cups water
- 1 tablespoon vanilla extract
- 1 cinnamon stick
- 1 tablespoon butter
- 1 cup raisins
- 3 tablespoons honey
- ½ cup heavy cream

### DIRECTIONS:

1. Add the water, rice, cinnamon stick, vanilla, and butter in the Instant Pot.
2. Secure the lid of the cooker and press the Manual function key.
3. Adjust the time to 20 minutes and cook at high pressure.
4. After the beep, release the pressure naturally and remove the lid.
5. Stir in honey, raisins, and cream.
6. Cook on Sauté function for 5 minutes.
7. Serve hot.

**NUTRITION:** calories: 438 | fat: 11.4g | protein: 5.0g | carbs: 83.5g | net carbs: 80.6g | fiber: 2.9g

---

## PUREED KALE CURRY

Preparation Time: 3 minutes

Cooking Time: 15 minutes

Servings: 2-3

### INGREDIENTS:

- 2 cups kale leaves, chopped
- 2 cups chicken broth
- 1 teaspoon garlic paste
- 2-inch ginger sliced, shredded
- ¼ teaspoon turmeric powder
- ¼ teaspoon salt
- 1 green chili
- 1 tablespoon coconut oil
- ½ cup water

### DIRECTIONS:

1. In a blender add kale with water and green chili, blend till puree.
2. Now heat oil in a pan and add ginger with garlic, sauté for 1 minute.
3. Add kale and fry for 5 minutes or its color is slightly changed.
4. Pour chicken broth and add salt, leave to cook on low heat for 15-20 minutes.
5. 5.Serve and enjoy.

**NUTRITION:** Calories 269.5 Total Fat 6.3 g Total Carbohydrate 48.5 g Protein 7.9 g

---

## PUREED GENERAL TSO'S CHICKEN THIGH

Preparation Time: 15 minutes

Cooking Time: 15 minutes

Servings: 2-3

### INGREDIENTS:

- Chicken thigh (10 oz., boneless, skinless, cubed)
- Soy Sauce (1/2 Tablespoon)
- Salt (1/4 teaspoon)
- Cornstarch (1/3 cup)
- Oil (1 Tablespoon)
- Ginger (3 slices, minced)
- Garlic (1 clove, diced)
- Red chilies (5, seeds removed)
- Scallion (2 stalks, white parts)
- Sauce
- Chinese rice vinegar (3 Tablespoons)
- Soy sauce (2 ½ Tablespoons)
- Dark soy sauce (1/2 Tablespoon)
- Hoisin sauce (1 teaspoon)
- Water (1/4 cup)
- Cornstarch (1 Tablespoon)

## DIRECTIONS

1. Cover meat in a container with salt and soy sauce; let it marinate for 15 minutes. Mix together the ingredients for the sauce and put aside till needed.
2. Heat oil and put cornstarch on chicken. Cook chicken until browned.
3. Remove from pot with a slotted spoon and place on paper towels to absorb excess oil.
4. Using another pan or wok, heat 1 ½ tablespoons of oil, then add ginger, chilies, and garlic.
5. Cook until chilies are fragrant. Put sauce into wok/pan and cook till sauce gets thick, then add chicken. Stir to combine and add scallions.
6. Add to a food processor and puree until smooth.
7. Serve hot.

**NUTRITION:** Calories 310 Total Fat 5 g Total Carbohydrate 57 g Protein 7 g

# RUSTIC BEEF RAGU PUREE

Preparation Time: 5 minutes

Cooking Time: 1 hours

Servings: 2-3

## INGREDIENTS:

- Beef (4 lbs.)
- Salt
- Pepper
- Olive Oil (2 Tbsp.)
- Onions (2, large, finely minced)
- Tomato Paste (1/4 Cup)
- Garlic (4 Cloves, minced)
- Lemon Water (1 Cup, Dry)
- Plum Tomatoes, (2 (796ml) Cans, Italian, crushed)
- Star Anise Pods (two)
- Bay Leaf (one)
- Cooked Polenta
- Parmesan Cheese (Shredded)

## DIRECTIONS

1. Trim and discard the excess fat from the top of the roast. Remove the excess liquid from it by patting it dry then proceed to season it with salt and pepper.
2. On medium setting heat the oil in a large pan. Now, for 3 to 4 minutes per side char the Beef, or char it until browned on every side, before transferring it off to a platter.
3. Set your oven to preheat at 250F and as it does, add in your seasoning of onions and tomato paste, occasionally stirring for 10 minutes or until the onion gets very soft. After this, garlic can be added while continuing to cooking for a minute or two.
4. Add lemon water while stirring. Immediately after, add the crushed tomatoes and tomato juice. Now, put back the roast into the pot and bring the mixture to a boil now by setting the heat to high.
5. The bay leaf and star anise should be wrapped in a cheesecloth pouch, dipped into the sauce and the pot covered. Move the pot now to your preheated oven for cooking for 3 hours. By this time your meat should be tender, falling away from its bone, at which time you may discard the bay leaf and star anise.
6. Remove your meat for cooling for about 5 minutes. Add the Beef into a food processor and blend until completely pureed. Return the pureed Beef to the pot, and you may throw out any bone.
7. Serve and enjoy.

**NUTRITION:** Calories 310 Total Fat 5 g Total Carbohydrate 57 g Protein 7 g

# CHEESY GRITS

Preparation Time:10 min

Cooking Time:10 min

Servings: 2-3

**INGREDIENTS:**

- 1 cup grits, uncooked
- 3 eggs, lightly beaten
- 1 cup cheddar cheese, shredded
- ¼ cup half-and-half

**DIRECTIONS**

1. Preparation time the grits according to the package directions

2. Meanwhile, in a small bowl, combine the beaten eggs with the cheese.
3. When the grits are almost done, stir 3 tablespoons of the hot grits into the egg mixture.
4. Add the egg mixture to the cooking time grits; whisk the egg mixture into the grits until the grits are smooth.
5. Add half-and-half; continue whisking until the grits are of desired consistency.

**NUTRITION** Calories 304.5 Total fat 9.6g carbohydrate 36.4g Protein 16.9g

# HIGH-PROTEIN PORRIDGE

Preparation Time:5 minutes

Cooking Time: 15 minutes

Servings: 2-3

**INGREDIENTS:**

- ¾ cup water
- ¼ raw steel cut oats
- 1 tablespoon raisins, no sugar added
- 1 tablespoon chopped walnuts
- 1 tablespoon creamy almond butter
- 1 tablespoon sugar-free strawberry jam

**DIRECTIONS:**

1. In a small saucepan over high heat, bring the water to a boil.

2. Stir in the oats and raisins. Reduce the heat to low and simmer, uncovered, for 20 minutes, stirring regularly, until the oats have thickened and absorbed the water. Remove from the heat.
3. Stir in the walnuts. Let the mixture rest for 1 minute.
4. Top with the almond butter and strawberry jam. Enjoy warm.
5. POST-OP TIP: I suggest waiting until you are at least six months post-op before adding it to your weekly breakfast rotation. Eat slowly, chew well, and stop when you feel full.

**NUTRITION:**(5½ ounces): Protein: 10g; Calories: 338; Fat: 16g; Carbohydrates: 43g; Fiber: 7g; Total sugar: 7g; Added sugar: 0g; Sodium: 6g

# MUSHROOM AND WILD RICE SOUP

Preparation Time:10 min

Cooking Time: 2 hours

Servings: 2-3

**INGREDIENTS:**

- Onion, white, chopped (1/2 piece)
- White wine (1/2 cup) or chicken broth, fat free, low sodium (1/2 cup)
- Thyme, dried (1/4 teaspoon)
- Carrots, chopped (1/4 cup)
- Milk, half and half, fat free (1 cup)
- Wild rice, cooked (1 cup)
- Olive oil, extra virgin (1 tablespoon)

- Celery, chopped (1/4 cup)
- White mushrooms, fresh, sliced (1 ½ cups)
- Chicken broth, fat free, low sodium (2 ½ cups)
- Flour (2 tablespoons)
- Black pepper, freshly ground (1/2 teaspoon)

**DIRECTIONS:**

1. Heat a stock pot on medium, then add the olive oil.
2. Stir in the chopped onion as well as carrots and celery. Cook for two to three min or until tender and fragrant.

3. Pour in the chicken broth and white wine. Add the mushrooms as well, then stir to combine. Cover and allow the mixture to get heated through.
4. Meanwhile, place the flour in a large bowl. Add the milk, pepper, and thyme; stir to combine. Add the cooked rice and toss until well-combined.

5. Transfer the rice mixture into the vegetable pot. Stir well before cooking time on medium until bubbly and thickened.

**NUTRITION:** Calories: 270kcal carbohydrates: 18.5g protein: 34.8g fat: 7.1g saturated fat: 0.7g polyunsaturated fat: 6.4g cholesterol: 75mg sodium: 994mg fiber: 1g

## BLACK BEAN AND PUMPKIN SOUP

Preparation Time:5 min

Cooking Time:15 min

Servings: 2-3

### INGREDIENTS:

- Onion, medium, chopped (1 piece)
- Black pepper, freshly ground (1/2 teaspoon)
- Pumpkin puree, canned (16 ounces)
- Cumin, ground (1 tablespoon)
- Tomatoes, canned, diced (1 cup)
- Olive oil, extra virgin (2 tablespoons)
- Garlic cloves, minced (4 pieces)
- Chili powder (1 teaspoon)
- Black beans, canned, rinsed, drained (30 ounces)
- Beef broth, low sodium (2 cups)

### DIRECTIONS:

1. Heat a soup kettle on medium after filling with the oil.
2. Add the garlic, onions, pepper, chili powder, and cumin. Stir and cook for about two to three min or until soft and fragrant.
3. Add the broth as well as pumpkin, tomatoes, and black beans. Stir to combine.
4. Allow the mixture to simmer, uncovered, for twenty-five min or until thickened to your desired consistency.
5. Remove from heat and process the black bean and pumpkin soup with an immersion blender.
6. Servings: and enjoy.

**NUTRITION:** Calories: 266kcal carbohydrates: 13g protein: 4g fat: 24g saturated fat: 21g sodium: 879mg potassium: 641mg fiber: 3g sugar: 4g vitamin a: 17726iu vitamin c: 23mg calcium: 71mg iron: 6mg

## GUAVA SMOOTHIE

Preparation Time: 5-7 minutes

Cooking Time: 2 minutes

Servings: 2-3

### INGREDIENTS:

- 1 cup guava, seeds removed, chopped
- 1 cup baby spinach, finely chopped
- 1 banana, peeled and sliced
- 1 tsp. fresh ginger, grated
- ½ medium-sized mango, peeled and chopped
- 2 cups water

### DIRECTIONS:

1. Peel the guava and cut in half. Scoop out the seeds and wash it. Cut into small pieces and set aside.
2. Rinse the baby spinach thoroughly under cold running water. Drain well and torn into small pieces. Set aside.
3. Peel the banana and chop into small chunks. Set aside.
4. Peel the mango and cut into small pieces. Set aside.
5. Now, combine guava, baby spinach, banana, ginger, and mango in a juicer and process until well combined. Gradually add water and blend until all combined and creamy.

6. Transfer to a serving glass and refrigerate for 20 minutes before serving.
7. Enjoy!

**NUTRITION:** Net carbs 39.1 g Fiber 7.8 g Fats 1.4 g Sugar 2 g Calories 166

## WATERMELON, CANTALOUPE AND MANGO SMOOTHIE

Preparation Time: 5 minutes;

Cooking Time: 0 minutes;

Servings: 4-5

### INGREDIENTS:

- ½ of a large mango, peeled
- ½ of burro banana, peeled
- ½ cup cantaloupe, peeled
- ½ cup amaranth greens
- ½ cup watermelon chunks

**Extra:**

- 1 cup soft jelly coconut water

### DIRECTIONS:

1. Plug in a high-speed food processor or blender and add all the Ingredients: in its jar.
2. Cover the blender jar with its lid and then pulse for 40 to 60 seconds until smooth.
3. Divide the drink between two glasses and then serve.

**NUTRITION:** 132 Calories; 1 g Fats; 3.5 g Protein; 30.1 g Carbohydrates; 3.2 g Fiber;

## BLACKBERRY & BANANA SMOOTHIE

Preparation Time: 5 minutes;

Cooking Time: 0 minutes;

Servings: 2-3

### INGREDIENTS:

- 1 burro banana, peeled
- ½ cup blackberries
- 2 dates, pitted
- 1 cup mango chunks
- ¼ cup walnut milk, unsweetened

**Extra:**

- ¾ cup of coconut water

### DIRECTIONS:

1. Plug in a high-speed food processor or blender and add all the Ingredients: in its jar.
2. Cover the blender jar with its lid and then pulse for 40 to 60 seconds until smooth.
3. Divide the drink between two glasses and then serve.

**NUTRITION:** 147.7 Calories; 0.7 g Fats; 5 g Protein; 34 g Carbohydrates; 4.1 g Fiber

## GREEN SMOOTHIE WITH RASPBERRIES

Preparation Time: 5 minutes;

Cooking Time: 5 minutes;

Servings: 2-3

### INGREDIENTS:

- 1 cup raspberries
- 1 cup kale leaves
- 1 tablespoon sea moss
- 2 tablespoons key lime juice
- 1 cup soft-jelly coconut milk

### DIRECTIONS:

1. Plug in a high-speed food processor or blender and add all the Ingredients: in its jar.
2. Cover the blender jar with its lid and then pulse for 40 to 60 seconds until smooth.
3. Divide the drink between two glasses and then serve.

**NUTRITION:** 151 Calories; 1.2 g Fats; 3 g Protein; 37 g Carbohydrates; 8 g Fiber;

## VEGGIE-FUL SMOOTHIE

Preparation Time: 5 minutes;

Cooking Time: 0 minutes;

Servings: 2-3

### INGREDIENTS:

- 1 pear, cored, deseeded
- ½ cup watercress
- ¼ of avocado, peeled
- ½ cup Romaine lettuce
- ½ of cucumber, peeled, deseeded

**Extra:**

- 1 tablespoon date
- ½ cup spring water

### DIRECTIONS:

1. Plug in a high-speed food processor or blender and add all the Ingredients: in its jar.
2. Cover the blender jar with its lid and then pulse for 40 to 60 seconds until smooth.
3. Divide the drink between two glasses and then serve.

**NUTRITION:** 145 Calories; 6 g Fats; 1 g Protein; 25 g Carbohydrates; 6 g Fiber;

## APPLE PIE SMOOTHIE

Preparation Time: 5 minutes;

Cooking Time: 0 minutes;

Servings: 2-3

### INGREDIENTS:

- ½ of a large apple, deseeded
- ¼ cup walnuts
- 2 figs
- 1 teaspoon Bromide Plus Powder

**Extra:**

- 1 tablespoon date

### DIRECTIONS:

1. Plug in a high-speed food processor or blender and add all the Ingredients: in its jar.
2. Cover the blender jar with its lid and then pulse for 40 to 60 seconds until smooth.
3. Divide the drink between two glasses and then serve.

**NUTRITION:** 170 Calories; 8 g Fats; 2 g Protein; 26 g Carbohydrates; 8 g Fiber

## BANANA ALMOND SMOOTHIE

Preparation Time: 5 minutes

Cooking Time: 2 minutes

Servings: 2-3

### INGREDIENTS:

- 15 almonds
- 1 cup unsweetened almond milk
- 1 apple, peeled
- 1 banana, frozen

### DIRECTIONS:

1. Add all ingredients into the blender and blend until smooth and creamy.
2. Serve and enjoy.

**NUTRITION:** Calories 190 Fat 5 g Carbohydrates 61 g Sugar 41 g Protein 14 g Cholesterol 18 mg

## PROTEIN SPINACH SHAKE

Preparation Time: 10 minutes

Cooking Time: 2 minutes

Servings: 2-3

### INGREDIENTS:

- 2/3 cup water
- ½ cup ice
- 5 drops liquid stevia
- ¼ cup vanilla protein powder
- ½ cup fat-free plain yogurt
- ½ tsp. vanilla extract
- 2 cups fresh spinach

### DIRECTIONS:

1. Add all ingredients into the blender and blend until smooth.
2. Serve and enjoy.

**NUTRITION:**Calories 54 Fat 0.9 g Carbohydrates 5.5 g Sugar 4.6 g Protein 4.4 g Cholesterol 4 mg

## FRESH LEMON CREAM SHAKE

Preparation Time: 5 minutes

Cooking Time: 2 minutes

Servings: 2-3

### INGREDIENTS:

- ½ cup ice cubes
- 2 tsp. lemon zest, grated
- ½ cup fat-free plain yogurt
- 1 scoop vanilla protein powder
- 5 oz. water
- 5 drops liquid stevia

### DIRECTIONS:

1. Add all ingredients into the blender and blend until smooth and creamy.
2. Serve and enjoy.

**NUTRITION:**Calories 175 Fat 0.1 g Carbohydrates 9.8 g Sugar 9 g Protein 33.1 g Cholesterol 4 mg

## AVOCADO BANANA SMOOTHIE

Preparation Time: 10 minutes

Cooking Time: 2 minutes

Servings: 2-3

### INGREDIENTS:

- ½ tsp. vanilla
- 1 tbsp. honey
- 2 cups unsweetened coconut milk
- 1 cup ice cubes
- 1 cup baby spinach
- ½ avocado
- 3 bananas

### DIRECTIONS:

1. Add all ingredients into the blender and blend until smooth and creamy.
2. Serve and enjoy.

**NUTRITION:**Calories 425 Fat 33 g Carbohydrates 33 g Sugar 19 g Protein 4 g Cholesterol 0 mg

## BANANA CHERRY SMOOTHIE

Preparation Time: 5 minutes

Cooking Time: 2 minutes

Servings: 2-3

### INGREDIENTS:

- ½ tsp. vanilla
- 2 tbsp. unsweetened cocoa powder
- 2 ½ tbsp. chia seeds
- 1 cup unsweetened almond milk
- 1 cup ice cubes
- 1 cup fresh spinach
- 1 banana

**DIRECTIONS:**

1. Add all ingredients into the blender and blend until smooth and creamy.

## SQUASH SOUP

Preparation Time: 5 minutes

Cooking Time: 15 minutes

Servings: 2-3

**INGREDIENTS:**

- 3 cups butternut squash, chopped
- 4 cups vegetable stock
- 3 garlic cloves, chopped
- 1 tbsp. olive oil
- 1 1/2 cups coconut milk
- 3/4 tbsp. curry powder
- 1/2 tsp. dried onion flakes
- 1 tsp. kosher salt

**DIRECTIONS:**

2. Serve and enjoy.

**NUTRITION:** Calories 135 Fat 5 g Carbohydrates 20 g Sugar 7 g Protein 4.6 g Cholesterol 0 mg

1. Add butternut squash, oil, onion flakes, curry powder, stock, garlic, and salt into a saucepan and bring to boil over medium-high heat.
2. Turn heat to medium and simmer for 20 minutes.
3. Puree the soup using immersion blender until smooth.
4. Return soup to the saucepan and stir in coconut milk and cook for 2-3 minutes.
5. Serve and enjoy.

**NUTRITION:** Calories 144 Fat 11 g Carbohydrates 10 g Sugar 2.5 g Protein 2 g Cholesterol 0 mg

## CREAMY AVOCADO SOUP

Preparation Time: 20 minutes

Cooking Time: 2 minutes

Servings: 2-3

**INGREDIENTS:**

- 2 avocados, peel and pitted
- 2 cups vegetable stock
- 1 tbsp. fresh lemon juice
- 3/4 cup heavy cream
- 2 tbsp. dry sherry
- Pepper
- Salt

**DIRECTIONS:**

1. Add avocado, lemon juice, sherry, and stock to the blender and blend until smooth.
2. Pour blended mixture into a bowl.
3. Add cream and stir well. Season with pepper and salt.
4. Serve and enjoy.

**NUTRITION:** Calories 102 Fat 9.5 g Carbohydrates 1.9 g Sugar 0.3 g Protein 2.4 g Cholesterol 27 mg

## CELERY SOUP

Preparation Time: 18 minutes

Cooking Time: 5 minutes

Servings: 2-3

**INGREDIENTS:**

- 5 celery stalks, chopped
- 3 cups vegetable stock
- 3 tbsp. almonds, chopped
- Pepper
- Salt

**DIRECTIONS:**

1. Add stock in a saucepan and bring to boil over high heat for 2 minutes.
2. Add celery and cook for 8 minutes.
3. Remove from heat and using immersion blender puree until smooth.

4. Add almonds and stir well.
5. Season with pepper and salt.
6. Serve and enjoy.

**NUTRITION:** Calories 80 Fat 6 g Carbohydrates 5 g Sugar 2 g Protein 3 g Cholesterol 0 mg

## CAULIFLOWER SOUP

Preparation Time: 35 minutes

Cooking Time: 10 minutes

Servings: 2-3

### INGREDIENTS:

- 1/2 head cauliflower, chopped
- 2 garlic cloves, minced
- 15 oz. vegetable stock
- 1/4 tsp. garlic powder
- 1 onion, diced
- 1 tbsp. olive oil
- 1/4 tsp. pepper
- 1/2 tsp. salt

### DIRECTIONS:

1. Heat oil in a saucepan over medium heat.
2. Add onion and garlic and sauté for 4-5 minutes.
3. Add cauliflower and stock and stir well. Bring to boil.
4. Cover and simmer for 15 minutes. Season with garlic powder, pepper, and salt.
5. Puree the soup using blender until smooth.
6. Serve and enjoy.

**NUTRITION:** Calories 40 Fat 2 g Carbohydrates 4 g Sugar 2 g Protein 3 g Cholesterol 0 mg

## AVOCADO MILK WHIP

Preparation Time: 10 minutes

Cooking Time: 0 minutes

Servings: 2-3

### INGREDIENTS:

- 1 avocado, peeled, pitted, diced
- 1 cup skimmed milk
- ½ cup non-fat cottage cheese
- ¼ cup fresh cilantro leaves, stems removed
- ½ teaspoon lime juice
- ¼ teaspoon garlic powder
- Chili powder, for garnish

### DIRECTIONS:

1. Put all ingredients in a blender and blend until smooth.
2. Divide the whip between two bowls and sprinkle with a dash of chili powder to serve.

**NUTRITION:** calories: 317 | total carbs: 26.6g | protein: 11.5g | total fat: 20.0g | sugar: 17.7g | fiber: 6.8g | sodium: 241mg

## BANANA AND KALE SMOOTHIE

Preparation Time: 5 minutes

Cooking Time: 0 minutes

Servings: 2-3

### INGREDIENTS:

- 2 cups unsweetened almond milk
- 2 cups kale, stemmed, leaves chopped
- 2 bananas, peeled
- 1 to 2 packets stevia, or to taste
- 1 teaspoon ground cinnamon
- 1 cup crushed ice

### DIRECTIONS:

 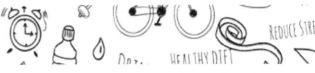
1. In a blender, combine the almond milk, kale, bananas, stevia, cinnamon, and ice. Blend until smooth.
2. Serve immediately.

**NUTRITION:** calories: 181 | total carbs: 37.0g | protein: 4.0g | total fat: 4.0g | sugar: 15.0g | fiber: 6.0g | sodium: 210mg

## BEEF PURÉE

Preparation Time: 30 minutes

Cooking Time: 2-5 hours

Servings: 2-3

### INGREDIENTS:

- 1 pound (454 g) beef tenderloin steak
- 1 teaspoon olive oil
- 1 teaspoon soy sauce
- ½ teaspoon salt, plus more to taste
- ½ teaspoon garlic powder
- ½ teaspoon onion powder
- ½ teaspoon dried rosemary, crushed
- ½ teaspoon dried parsley
- ¼ teaspoon freshly ground black pepper, plus more to taste
- Beef stock, as needed

### DIRECTIONS:

1. Pat the steak dry with paper towels and brush with olive oil and soy sauce. Mix salt, garlic powder, onion powder, rosemary, parsley and pepper and rub over steak. Cook the steak in a slow cooker until cooked through and the internal temperature reaches 145°F (63°C), 8 to 10 hours at the low setting or 4 to 5 hours at the high setting.
2. Remove the steak from slow cooker, reserving the cooking juices. Put the steak in a covered container and refrigerate until chilled through, about 2 hours.
3. Cut the chilled steak into 1-inch cubes. Put about 1 cup steak cubes in a food processor and blend until fine and powdery. Add about ¼ cup reserved cooking juices plus stock as needed and process until smooth. Repeat with remaining steak cubes.
4. Season the puréed steak with salt and pepper and stir until thoroughly combined.
5. Serve immediately.

**NUTRITION:** calories: 168 | total carbs: 1g | protein: 23.3g | total fat: 7.9g | sugar: 0.3g | fiber: 0.2g | sodium: 410mg

## BLUEBERRY AND SPINACH SMOOTHIE

Preparation Time: 5 minutes

Cooking Time: 2 minutes

Servings: 2-3

### INGREDIENTS:

- 2 cups blueberries
- 3 cups chopped fresh spinach
- ½ cup chopped fresh coriander
- Juice of 1 lemon
- 1-inch fresh ginger, grated
- 2 cups water

### DIRECTIONS:

1. Put all the ingredients in the blender, mix for 2 minutes or until smooth.
2. Serve immediately.

**NUTRITION:** calories: 121 | total carbs: 30.0g | protein: 1.6g | total fat: 0.6g | sugar: 26.6g | fiber: 2.6g | sodium: 25mg

## BROCCOLI PURÉE

Preparation Time: 30 minutes

Cooking Time: 5 minutes

Servings: 2-3

### INGREDIENTS:

- 1 pound (454 g) fresh broccoli, cut into florets

- ½ cup water
- ½ teaspoon salt, plus more to taste
- 1 teaspoon butter
- 1 teaspoon lemon juice
- ½ teaspoon onion powder
- Freshly ground black pepper, to taste

**DIRECTIONS:**

1. Mix the broccoli florets, water and ½ teaspoon salt in a medium saucepan and bring to a simmer. Reduce heat, cover the pan and simmer until the broccoli is tender, 5 to 10 minutes.

2. Drain the broccoli, reserving the cooking water. Add the butter, lemon juice and onion powder, season with salt and pepper and let cool.

3. Put about 1 cup broccoli florets and ¼ cup cooking water in a food processor and mix until smooth. Repeat with remaining broccoli.

4. Serve immediately.

**NUTRITION:**calories: 28 | total carbs: 4.3g | protein: 2.4g | total fat: 0.9g | sugar: 1.g | fiber: 2.3g | sodium: 212mg

## EASY CHOCOLATE AND ORANGE PUDDING

Preparation Time: 5 minutes

Cooking Time: 5 minutes

Servings: 2-3

### INGREDIENTS:

- 1 package sugar-free instant chocolate pudding mix
- ¼ cup chocolate protein powder
- 2 cups low-fat milk
- 1 tablespoon cocoa powder
- 1 teaspoon orange extract

### DIRECTIONS:

1. In a small bowl, whisk the pudding and protein powders together with the milk for 2 minutes.

2. Add the cocoa powder and orange extract, and mix for 3 more minutes before serving.

**NUTRITION:**calories: 111 | total carbs: 15.0g | protein: 10.0g | total fat: 2.0g | sugar: 6.0g | fiber: 1.0g | sodium: 380mg

## HERBED CHICKEN PURÉE

Preparation Time: 30 minutes

Cooking Time: 15 minutes

Servings: 2-3

### INGREDIENTS:

- 2 (8-ounce / 227-g) boneless skinless chicken breasts
- 2 bay leaves
- ¾ teaspoon salt, divided
- ¾ teaspoon ground sage
- ½ teaspoon ground thyme
- ¼ teaspoon ground marjoram
- ¼ teaspoon ground rosemary
- ¼ teaspoon freshly ground black pepper
- Dash of nutmeg

### DIRECTIONS:

1. Put the chicken breasts, bay leaves, and 1/2 teaspoon in a medium saucepan, add enough cold water to cover and bring to boil. Reduce the heat, cover and simmer gently until chicken is cooked through and

the internal temperature reaches at least 165°F (74°C), 20 to 25 minutes.

2. Remove the chicken breasts from broth. Strain and reserve the broth. Put chicken in a covered container and refrigerate until chilled through, about 2 hours.

3. Cut the chilled chicken breasts into 1-inch cubes. Put about 1 cup chicken cubes in a food processor and pulse until fine and powdery. Add about ¼ cup reserved broth and process until smooth. Repeat with remaining chicken cubes.

4. Mix the sage, thyme, marjoram, rosemary, pepper and nutmeg with remaining salt, sprinkle over the puréed chicken and stir until thoroughly combined.

5. Serve immediately.

**NUTRITION:** calories: 92 | total carbs: 0.2g | protein: 17.1g | total fat: 2g | sugar: 0g | fiber: 0.1g | sodium: 325mg

## MATCHA MANGO SMOOTHIE

Preparation Time: 5 minutes

Cooking Time: 0 minutes

Servings: 2-3

### INGREDIENTS:

- 2 cups cubed mango
- 2 tablespoons matcha powder
- 2 teaspoons turmeric powder
- 2 cups almond milk
- 2 tablespoons honey
- 1 cup crushed ice

### DIRECTIONS:

1. In a blender, combine the mango, matcha, turmeric, almond milk, honey, and ice. Blend until smooth.
2. Serve immediately.

**NUTRITION:** calories: 285 | total carbs: 68.0g | protein: 4.0g | total fat: 3.0g | sugar: 63.0g | fiber: 6.0g | sodium: 94mg

## RICOTTA PEACH FLUFF

Preparation Time: 10 minutes

Cooking Time: 0 minutes

Servings: 2-3

### INGREDIENTS:

- ¼ cup ricotta cheese
- 1 ripe peach, diced
- 2 tablespoons skim milk

### DIRECTIONS:

1. Purée ricotta, diced peach and milk in a blender until smooth.
2. Serve immediately

**NUTRITION:** calories: 355 | total carbs: 54.0g | protein: 17.9g | total fat: 8.7g | sugar: 50.0g | fiber: 2.0g | sodium: 183mg

## SIMPLE APPLESAUCE

Preparation Time: 10 minutes

Cooking Time: 8 minutes

Servings: 2-3

### INGREDIENTS:

- 2 medium apples (peeled, cored, sliced)
- ¼ cup water, plus more if needed
- Dash cinnamon
- Dash nutmeg

### DIRECTIONS:

1. Put all ingredients in a small saucepan and heat to simmer. Cook, stirring frequently, until apples are very soft and falling apart, about 15 minutes.
2. Purée applesauce with an immersion blender until very smooth, adding more water if necessary.
3. Serve immediately or refrigerate applesauce until chilled through, about 1 hour, before serving.

**NUTRITION:** calories: 63 | total carbs: 16.8g | protein: 0.3g | total fat: 0.2g | sugar: 12.6g | fiber: 2.9g | sodium: 0mg

# CHAPTER 5. SOFT FOOD RECIPES

### BEST CHOCOLATE PORRIDGE

Preparation Time: 1 minute

Cooking Time: 3 minutes

Servings: 2-3

**INGREDIENTS:**

- Small square dark unsweetened chocolate
- 1 tablespoon low-calorie sweetener
- 1 tablespoon chocolate protein powder
- 3 tablespoons porridge oats
- 1 cup skimmed milk

**DIRECTIONS:**

1. Add chocolate, protein powder, milk, and oats to a jug. Mix well and transfer to microwave container, cook for 2 minutes. Stir and cook for 20-30 seconds more. Mix in your desired sweetener and spoon mixture into a serving bowl.
2. Top with a couple of blackberries and a bit of chopped chocolate.
3. Enjoy!

**NUTRITION:**Calories 324, Fat 5, Carbs 12, Protein 8, Sodium 177

### CHOCOLATE CHIA PUDDING

Preparation Time: 10 minutes

Cooking Time: 0 minutes

Servings: 2-3

**INGREDIENTS:**

- 2 cups unsweetened soy milk
- 10 drops liquid stevia
- ¼ cup unsweetened cocoa powder
- ¼ teaspoon ground cinnamon
- ¼ teaspoon vanilla extract
- ½ cup chia seeds
- ½ cup fresh raspberries, for garnish

**DIRECTIONS:**

1. Take a small-sized bowl and whisk in soy milk, stevia, cocoa powder, cinnamon, vanilla and mix well until combined.
2. Stir in chia seeds.
3. Divide the mixture between 4 small dishes.
4. Cover and let it chill for 1 hour.
5. Once done, garnish with raspberries, enjoy!

**NUTRITION:**Calories 312, Fat 4, Carbs 17, Protein 8, Sodium 221

### LEMON-BLACKBERRY FROZEN YOGURT

Preparation Time: 10 minutes

Cooking Time: 0 minutes

Servings: 2-3

**INGREDIENTS:**

- 4 cups frozen blackberries
- ½ cup low-fat plain Greek yogurt
- 1 lemon, juiced
- 2 teaspoons liquid stevia

- Fresh mint leaves, for garnish

**Directions:**

1. Take your food processor and ad blackberries, yogurt, lemon juice, stevia and blend well until smooth.

2. Serve immediately and enjoy with a garnish of fresh mint leaves.

**NUTRITION:**Calories: 68, Total Fat: 0g, Saturated Fat: 0g, Protein: 3g, Carbs: 15g, Fiber: 5g

## CREAMY CAULIFLOWER DISH

Preparation Time: 10 minutes

Cooking Time: 5 minutes

Servings: 2-3

**INGREDIENTS:**

- ½ teaspoon pepper
- 4 teaspoon extra virgin olive oil
- ½ teaspoon garlic salt
- 1 teaspoon salted butter
- 1/3 cup low-fat buttermilk
- 3 cloves garlic
- Large head of cauliflower

**DIRECTIONS:**

1. Break your cauliflower into small florets and transfer to a large microwave proof bowl, add garlic and a quarter of water.
2. Microwave for 5 minutes until cauliflower is tender.
3. Use a garlic press and crush garlic cloves, add to food processor and add to cauliflower.
4. Add pepper, garlic salt, butter, two teaspoons olive oil, buttermilk.
5. Process well until creamy and smooth.
6. Drizzle remaining olive oil on top and enjoy!

**NUTRITION:**Calories: 113, Total Fat: 6g, Saturated Fat: 2g, Protein: 5g, Carbs: 13g, Fiber: 3g

## BEETROOT AND BUTTERBEAN HUMMUS

Preparation Time: 5 minutes

Cooking Time: 0 minutes

Servings: 2-3

**INGREDIENTS:**

- Salt and pepper as needed
- 1 tablespoon extra-virgin olive oil
- 2 tablespoons Fat-Free Greek yogurt
- Bunch of chives, chopped
- 1-2 cloves garlic, crushed
- 14 ounces butterbeans, drained and rinsed
- 8 ounces cooked beetroot

**DIRECTIONS:**

1. Dice beetroot and cut into small cubes.
2. Add butterbeans in a food processor and season with salt, pepper, yogurt, oil, chives, and garlic.
3. Blitz until the mixture is a nice puree.
4. Fold in diced beetroot and blitz gently.
5. Serve and enjoy!

**NUTRITION:**Calories: 80, Total Fat: 2g, Saturated Fat: 0g, Protein: 4.2g, Carbs: 10g, Fiber: 0.

## RAISIN AND OATS MUG CAKES

Preparation Time: 10 minutes

Cooking Time: 1 minute

Servings: 2-3

**INGREDIENTS:**

- 1 and ½ tablespoons flour
- 1 and ½ tablespoons almond milk
- ½ tablespoon raisins

- ¼ teaspoon baking powder
- 1/16 teaspoon salt
- ½ tablespoons canola oil
- 1/8 teaspoons baking soda
- 1/8 teaspoons vanilla extract
- 1/8 teaspoons hazelnut extract
- ¾ tablespoons oats

**NUTRITION:**Calories: 185, Total Fat: 1.7g, Saturated Fat: 1g, Protein: 8g, Carbs: 39g, Fiber: 10g

- 1 teaspoon lemon juice
- ¼ teaspoon baking powder

**DIRECTIONS:**

1. Whisk in all ingredients in a microwave-proof mug and cook on high for 1 minute.
2. Let it cool, serve and enjoy!

## NO-BAKE PEANUT BUTTER PROTEIN BITES AND DARK CHOCOLATE

Preparation Time: 20 minutes + chill time

Cooking Time: 0 minutes

Servings: 2-3

### INGREDIENTS:

- 1 cup old fashioned rolled oats
- 1 cup vanilla protein powder
- ¾ cup smooth natural peanut butter
- 2 tablespoons ground flaxseed
- 1 tablespoon ground flaxseed
- 1 tablespoon chia seeds
- 1 teaspoon vanilla extract
- ¼ cup dark chocolate chips

- ¾ teaspoons stevia baking blend
- 1 tablespoon water

### DIRECTIONS:

1. Take a bowl and mix in oats, protein powder, peanut butter, flaxseed, chia seeds, vanilla, chocolate chips, stevia, and water.
2. Let it chill for 30 minutes.
3. Roll the mixture into 25 balls, eat and enjoy!

**NUTRITION:**Calories: 181; Total Fat: 10g; Saturated Fat: 0g; Protein: 11g; Carbs: 11g; Fiber: 3g

## EGG WHITE SCRAMBLE

Preparation Time: 5 minutes

Cooking Time: 5 minutes

Servings: 2-3

### INGREDIENTS:

- 1/4 cup non-fat cottage cheese
- 2 egg whites (lightly beaten)
- Nonstick cooking spray
- Pinch dried herbs (such as oregano or basil)
- Salt and freshly ground black pepper, to taste

### DIRECTIONS:

1. In a medium bowl, mash cottage cheese with a fork to break up curds. Add egg whites and beat until smooth.
2. Spray a small nonstick skillet with cooking spray and heat over medium heat. Add egg mixture, sprinkle with herbs and stir gently until cooked through, 4 to 5 minutes.
3. Mash cooked egg mixture with a fork to desired consistency, season to taste with salt and pepper and serve immediately. Enjoy!

**NUTRITION:**Calories: 85; Total Fat: 1g; Saturated Fat: 1g; Protein: 15g; Carbs: 2g; Fiber: 0g; Sugar: 0g

## HAM & SWISS EGGS

Preparation Time: 5 minutes

Cooking Time: 5 minutes

Servings: 2-3

### INGREDIENTS:

- teaspoon butter
- 4 eggs (lightly beaten)
- tablespoons skim milk
- Salt and freshly ground black pepper, to taste
- 1/4 cup shredded Swiss cheese
- 1/4 cup finely minced cooked ham

### DIRECTIONS:

1. Whisk eggs and milk until thoroughly combined and season to taste with salt and pepper. Melt butter in a medium nonstick skillet over medium heat and add egg mixture. Cook and stir until eggs are completely set and cooked through, 5 to 6 minutes.
2. Add cheese and ham to eggs and stir until combined and heated through. Season eggs to taste with salt and pepper and serve immediately. Enjoy!

NUTRITION:Calories: 238; Total Fat: 16g; Saturated Fat: 7g; Protein: 20g; Carbs: 2g; Fiber: 0g; Sugar: 0g

## PEANUT BUTTER CUP SMOOTHIES

Preparation Time: 10 minutes

Cooking Time: 0 minutes

Servings: 2-3

### INGREDIENTS:

- 1/2 cups skim milk
- 1/2 cup plain Greek yogurt
- tablespoons creamy natural peanut butter
- tablespoons sifted unsweetened cocoa powder
- 8 to 10 ice cubes

### DIRECTIONS:

1. Place all ingredients in a blender container and pulse until thoroughly blended and smooth.
2. Pour into 2 large glasses to serve. Enjoy!

NUTRITION:Calories: 175; Total Fat: 9g; Saturated Fat: 2g; Protein: 11g; Carbs: 15g; Fiber: 3g; Sugar: 11g

## BERRY CHEESECAKE SMOOTHIES

Preparation Time: 10 minutes

Cooking Time: 0 minutes

Servings: 2-3

### INGREDIENTS:

- 8 to 10 ice cubes
- cup mixed berries
- tablespoons cream cheese
- cups skim milk
- 1/4 teaspoon vanilla extract

### DIRECTIONS:

1. Place all ingredients in a blender container and pulse until thoroughly blended and smooth.
2. Pour into 2 large glasses to serve. Enjoy!

NUTRITION:Calories: 182; Total Fat: 5g; Saturated Fat: 3g; Protein: 10g; Carbs: 21g; Fiber: 3g; Sugar17g

## TROPICAL PORRIDGE

Preparation Time: 5 minutes

Cooking Time: 5 minutes

Servings: 2-3

### INGREDIENTS:

- cup coconut milk
- tablespoons farina breakfast porridge mix (such as Cream of Wheat Malt-O-Meal)
- 1/2 cup diced ripe mango
- 1 small banana (diced)

### DIRECTIONS:

1. Heat coconut milk to a simmer in a small saucepan over medium heat. Whisk farina into milk and stir until smooth.

2. Reduce heat and simmer, uncovered, until porridge is thickened, about 2 minutes. Remove porridge from heat and stir in mango and banana to serve. Enjoy!

**NUTRITION:** Calories: 172; Total Fat: 3g; Saturated Fat: 3g; Protein: 3g; Carbs: 34g; Fiber: 3g Sugar: 15g

## PORRIDGE WITH BERRIES

Preparation Time: 5 minutes

Cooking Time: 5 minutes

Servings: 2-3

### INGREDIENTS:

- 1. cup water
- 1/2 cup frozen mixed berries
- 1 tablespoon lemon juice
- 3 tablespoons farina breakfast porridge mix (such as Cream of Wheat or Malt-O-Meal)

### DIRECTIONS:

1. Mix water, berries and lemon juice in a small saucepan and heat to a boil over medium heat, stirring occasionally, gently crushing berries to desired consistency.
2. Whisk farina into saucepan and stir until smooth.
3. Reduce heat and simmer, uncovered, until porridge is thickened, about 2 minutes, stirring occasionally. Serve immediately and enjoy!

**NUTRITION:** Calories: 95; Total Fat: 0g; Saturated Fat: 0g; Protein: 3g; Carbs: 20g; Fiber: 4g; Sugar: 5g

## STRAWBERRIES WITH WHIPPED YOGURT

Preparation Time: 10 minutes

Cooking Time: 0 minutes

Servings: 2-3

### INGREDIENTS:

- 1. cup sliced strawberries
- 1. cup (8 ounces) plain Greek yogurt
- 2 tablespoons heavy cream

### DIRECTIONS:

1. Pulse strawberries in a food processor or blender as necessary until mashed or pureed to desired consistency and set aside.
2. In a medium bowl with tall sides, beat yogurt and cream with an electric hand mixer until thickened and stiff peaks form, about 5 minutes.
3. Spoon strawberries into two bowls, top with whipped yogurt and serve immediately. Enjoy!

**NUTRITION:** Calories: 210; Total Fat: 16g; Saturated Fat: 10g; Protein: 5g; Carbs: 14g; Fiber: 2g; Sugar: 12g

## GAZPACHO

Preparation Time: 15 minutes + 2 hours refrigerating

Cooking Time: 5 minutes

Servings: 2-3

### INGREDIENTS:

- 2 tablespoons vegetable oil
- small red bell pepper (diced)
- 1 small yellow onion (diced)

- garlic cloves (minced)
- large fresh ripe tomatoes (peeled, diced)
- 1 small cucumber (peeled, diced)
- 1 tablespoon lime juice
- 1 tablespoon balsamic vinegar
- 1 tablespoon chopped fresh basil leaves
- 1 teaspoon kosher salt, plus more to taste
- 1/2 teaspoon ground cumin
- Freshly ground black pepper, to taste

## DIRECTIONS:

1. In a medium saucepan, heat oil over medium heat and sauté bell pepper and onion until softened, about 5 minutes, stirring occasionally. Add garlic and sauté about 1 minute more, stirring constantly.
2. Remove pan from heat and stir in tomatoes, cucumber, lime juice, vinegar, basil, salt and cumin and season to taste with pepper.
3. If desired, pour mixture into a blender container and pulse to desired consistency, or use an immersion blender.
4. Refrigerate soup until chilled through, about 2 hours. Serve and enjoy!

**NUTRITION:** Calories: 124; Total Fat: 8g; Saturated Fat: 5g; Protein: 2g; Carbs: 14g; Fiber: 3g; Sugar: 2g

## CREAM OF CHICKEN SOUP

Preparation Time: 30 minutes

Cooking Time: 25 minutes

Servings: 2-3

## INGREDIENTS:

- 2 boneless skinless chicken breasts (about 8 ounces each)
- 6 cups water
- onion (quartered)
- bay leaves
- 1 teaspoon garlic salt
- cups chopped mixed vegetables (such as onions, carrots, celery, green beans or bell peppers)
- Salt and freshly ground black pepper, to taste
- tablespoons butter
- tablespoons flour
- 2 cups skim milk

## DIRECTIONS:

1. Place chicken breasts, water, onion, bay leaves and garlic salt in a large saucepan or stock pot and heat to a boil, skimming foam as necessary. Reduce heat, cover and simmer until chicken is cooked through, about 30 minutes.
2. Remove chicken breasts from broth. Strain broth, discarding solids.
3. Add vegetables to broth, season to taste with salt and pepper and heat to a boil. Reduce heat, cover and simmer until vegetables are tender, about 20 minutes.
4. Meanwhile, cut or shred chicken into bite-size pieces and set aside. Melt butter in a small nonstick skillet. Sprinkle flour over butter and whisk until smooth. Add milk to skillet in a thin stream, whisking constantly. Heat milk mixture to a simmer, whisking occasionally. Simmer for 2 minutes, whisking constantly.
5. Add milk mixture to broth and whisk to combine. Add chicken to soup and stir until heated through. Season soup to taste with salt and pepper and serve. Enjoy!

**NUTRITION:** Calories: 167; Total Fat: 8g; Saturated Fat: 4g; Protein: 15g; Carbs: 9g; Fiber: 1g; Sugar: 5g

## MUSHROOM SOUP WITH BRIE

Preparation Time: 15 minutes

Cooking Time: 15 minutes

Servings: 2-3

## INGREDIENTS:

- 2 tablespoons butter

- 2 packages (8 ounces) baby bella mushrooms (sliced)
- onion (julienned)
- garlic cloves (minced)
- 1 teaspoon dried thyme
- 1/2 cup white wine
- tablespoons flour
- cups chicken stock
- 3 cups skim milk
- ounces Brie (rind removed as necessary)

### DIRECTIONS:

1. Melt butter in a large saucepan and sauté mushrooms and onion until softened and caramelized, 8 to 10 minutes, stirring frequently. Add garlic and thyme sauté about 1 minute more, stirring constantly. Add wine and stir to deglaze pan.
2. Sprinkle flour into saucepan and stir to coat. Add broth and heat to a boil, stirring occasionally. Reduce heat and simmer soup for about 10 minutes, stirring occasionally.
3. Add milk to soup and heat to a simmer. Stir Brie into soup and stir until melted. Remove soup from heat and process with an immersion blender to desired consistency. Serve immediately and enjoy!

**NUTRITION:**Calories: 229; Total Fat: 11g; Saturated Fat: 6g; Protein: 14g; Carbs: 18g; Fiber: 1g; Sugar: 11g

## CARROT PUDDING

Preparation Time: 10 minutes

Cooking Time: 8 minutes

Servings: 2-3

### INGREDIENTS:

- 2/3 cup carrot puree
- 1 teaspoon vanilla paste
- 1 teaspoon lemon zest
- 4 cups of coconut milk
- Cornstarch (a mixture of 2 tablespoons cornstarch and 4 tablespoons water)
- 1 whole egg

### DIRECTIONS:

1. Add carrot and milk in a saucepan and place it over low heat, cover and cook until tiny bubbles appear.
2. Whisk egg, cornstarch slurry, lemon zest in a bowl and add into the pan in a steady stream.
3. Cover and cook for 15 minutes more.
4. Divide between dessert bowls and enjoy!

**NUTRITION:**Calories: 159; Total Fat: 10g; Saturated Fat: 2g; Protein: 4g; Carbs: 18g; Fiber: 3g

## FANCY SCRAMBLED EGGS

Preparation Time: 5 minutes

Cooking Time: 5 minutes

Servings: 2-3

### INGREDIENTS:

- 4 whole eggs
- 1/8 teaspoon salt
- 1/8 teaspoon pepper
- 2 tablespoons olive oil
- 2 tablespoons red bell pepper, chopped
- 1 garlic clove, chopped
- 1 and ½ teaspoons chives, chopped

### DIRECTIONS:

1. Take a bowl and beat eggs, pepper, and salt.
2. Take a large skillet and place it over medium heat, add oil, red bell pepper, garlic and cook for 5 minutes.
3. Add egg mixture and chives to skillet.
4. Cook and stir over low heat until eggs are cooked.

**NUTRITION:** 199; Total Fat: 15g; Saturated Fat: 2g; Protein: 13g; Carbs: 2g; Fiber: 0g

## YOGURT CRÈME BRULEE CUSTARD

Preparation Time: 10 minutes

Cooking Time: 0 minutes

Servings: 2-3

### INGREDIENTS:

- 2 cups thick Greek yogurt
- 1 cup strawberries puree

### DIRECTIONS:

1. Take a bowl and add strawberries puree and yogurt.
2. Divide the mixture between four ramekins.
3. Serve and enjoy!

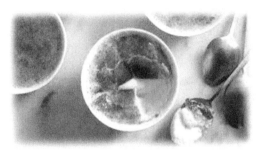

**NUTRITION:** Calories: 357; Total Fat: 27g; Saturated Fat: 4g; Protein: 6g; Carbs: 22g; Fiber: 4g

## BBQ'D BAKED BEANS

Preparation Time: 10 minutes

Cooking Time: 30 minutes

Servings: 2-3

### INGREDIENTS:

- 1 yellow onion, chopped
- 5 garlic cloves, minced
- ¼ pound potatoes, peeled and diced
- 6 cups of water
- 1 cup BBQ sauce
- 2 tablespoons spicy brown mustard
- 2 tablespoons adobo sauce
- Splash of Guinness
- 2 teaspoons salt
- 1 teaspoon pepper

### DIRECTIONS:

1. Wash beans thoroughly and soak overnight.
2. Set your oven to pre-heat and add potatoes to the oven, let them brown.
3. When brown, in a pan, add onions and Sauté until tender.
4. Keep Sautéing and add garlic, cook for 1 minute.
5. Pour beans, water, and cover, cook on low for 60 minutes until beans are tender.
6. Add a bit of BBQ sauce, adobo sauce, mustard salt, pepper, and stir.
7. Remove cover and let it simmer until sauce thickens and beans are cooked thoroughly.

**NUTRITION:** Calories: 70; Total Fat: 1g; Saturated Fat: 0g; Protein: 3g; Carbs: 14g; Fiber: 3g

# CHAPTER 6. BREAKFAST

## CHEESE-FILLED ACORN SQUASH

Preparation Time:10 min

Cooking Time:50 min

Servings: 2-3

### INGREDIENTS:

- Tofu, firm (1 pound)
- Basil (1 teaspoon)
- Black pepper, freshly ground (1 pinch)
- Onion, chopped finely (1 teaspoon)
- Garlic powder (1 teaspoon)
- Cheddar cheese, reduced fat, shredded (1 cup)
- Acorn squash, halved, seeded (2 pieces)
- Celery, diced (1 cup)
- Mushrooms, fresh, sliced (1 cup)
- Oregano (1 teaspoon)
- Salt (1/8 teaspoon)
- Tomato sauce (8 ounces)

### DIRECTIONS:

1. Set the oven at 350 degrees to preheat.
2. Arrange the acorn squash pieces, with their cut-sides facing down, at the bottom of a glass dish.
3. Place in the microwave oven and cook for about twenty min or until softened. Set aside.
4. Heat a saucepan (nonstick) on medium, then add the tofu (sliced into cubes). Cook until browned before stirring in the onion and celery. Cook for two min or until the onion is translucent.
5. Add the mushrooms. Stir to combine and cook for an additional two to three min. Pour in the tomato sauce as well as the dry seasonings.
6. Give everything a good stir, then spoon equal portions of the mixture inside the acorn squash pieces.
7. Cover and place in the oven to cook for about fifteen min. Uncover and top with the cheese before returning to the oven. Cook for five more min or until the cheese is melted and bubbling.

**NUTRITION:** Calories: 328kcal carbohydrates: 47.5g protein: 16.9g fat: 10.8g saturated fat: 5.8g polyunsaturated fat: 5g cholesterol: 42mg sodium: 557mg fiber: 7.7g sugar: 5.9g

## CHEESY SPINACH BAKE

Preparation Time:5 min

Cooking Time:35 min

Servings: 2-3

### INGREDIENTS:

- Eggs, whole (2 pieces)
- Parmesan cheese (1/2 cup)
- Cottage cheese, fat-free/ low fat (2 cups)
- Spinach, frozen, thawed, drained (10 ounces)

### DIRECTIONS:

1. Set the oven to 350 degrees to preheat. Meanwhile, line a baking pan (8x8) with parchment paper.

2. Place all ingredients in a large bowl. Stir to combine. Pour the cheesy spinach mixture into the preparation time bed pan. Place in the oven to bake for twenty to thirty min or until the cheese on top is bubbling.

3. Remove from the oven and allow to cool for five min.

4. Serve with sprinkled with garlic, salt, and pepper. Enjoy.

**NUTRITION:** 1g calories: 292kcal carbohydrates: 4.5g protein: 26g fat: 19.1g saturated fat: 7.2g monounsaturated fat: 11.9g cholesterol: 545mg sodium: 735mg fiber: 2g

## GREEK YOGURT, GRANOLA, AND BERRY PARFAIT

Preparation Time:10 minutes

Cooking Time: 15 minutes or Less

Servings: 2-3

### INGREDIENTS:

- ½ cup nonfat plain Greek yogurt
- 1 tablespoon rolled oats
- ¼ cup fresh blueberries
- ¼ cup fresh raspberries
- 1 tablespoon chopped walnuts
- 1 tablespoon chopped pecans
- 1 teaspoon honey

### DIRECTIONS:

1. Place the yogurt in a 6-ounce glass.
2. Top with the oats, blueberries, raspberries, walnuts, and pecans. Drizzle the honey on top. Enjoy immediately.
3. STORAGE TIP: You can prepare your own granola with rolled oats and your favorite nuts, as well as additional goodies such as coconut flakes, dried fruit, or fruit chips. Store it in an airtight container in a dry, dark place for up to 3 months. Use it in this parfait, a smoothie, or as a snack on its own.

**NUTRITION:(8 OUNCES):** Protein: 16g; Calories: 245; Fat: 11g; Carbohydrates: 25g; Fiber: 5g; Total sugar: 21g; Added sugar: 6g; Sodium: 46g

## EGGS FLORENTINE

Preparation Time:10 min

Cooking Time:10 min

Servings: 2-3

### INGREDIENTS:

- 2 large eggs (2 large)
- Extra virgin olive oil (1 tbsp., unfiltered)
- Egg fast alfredo sauce (5 tbsp.)
- Organic parmigiana Reggiano wedge (1 tbsp., divided)
- Organic baby spinach (3 grams)
- Red pepper flakes (1 pinch)

### DIRECTIONS

1. Set oven rack in the top groove nearest to the broiler. Set broiler to preheat.
2. Place olive oil in a non-stick skillet and put to heat over medium high heat.
3. Gently, fry eggs over medium flame, until egg whites are opaque but the yolk still runny. This takes roughly 4 min. Do not turn over eggs.
4. Prepare casserole in the meantime. Dribble some olive oil in each casserole container or spray with cooking time spray (olive oil).

5. In the bottom of the casserole, spread half of the alfredo sauce. Slide gently, the half-done egg atop sauce.
6. Spread leftover alfredo sauce and half of the parmesan cheese over eggs.
7. Set casserole under the broiler and broil for 2-3 min or until the eggs have formed and the top has bubbly golden spots.

8. Remove from broiler and top with thinly sliced (julienne) baby spinach leaves, unused parmesan cheese and a dash of red pepper flakes. Servings: instantly.

NUTRITION: Calories 529 Total fat 3g Total carbohydrate 3 g Protein 29g

## MEXICAN SCRAMBLED EGGS

Preparation Time:10 min

Cooking Time:5 min

Servings: 2-3

### INGREDIENTS:

- Eggs (6, lightly beaten)
- Tomato (1, diced)
- Cheese (3 oz., shredded)
- Butter (1 tbsp., for frying)

### DIRECTIONS

1. Set a large skillet with butter over medium heat and allow to melt.
2. Add tomatoes and green onions then cook, while stirring, until fragrant (about 3 min).
3. Add eggs, and continue to cook, while stirring, until almost set (about 2 min)
4. Add cheese, and season to taste continue cooking time until the cheese melts (about another minute).

NUTRITION: Calories 239 Total fat 3.7g

## SPINACH OMELET

Preparation Time:10 min

Cooking Time:10 min

Servings: 2-3

### INGREDIENTS:

- 2 tbsp olive oil
- 1 cup spinach, chopped
- 1 cup swiss chard, chopped
- 3 eggs 1 tsp garlic powder
- ½ tsp sea salt ¼ tsp red pepper flakes

### DIRECTIONS

1. Grease the pressure cooker's bottom with 2 tablespoons of olive oil.

2. Press beans/lentils button and add greens. Stir-fry for 5 min. Remove from the cooker and set aside.
3. Whisk together eggs, garlic powder, salt, and red pepper flakes. Pour the mixture into the stainless-steel insert.
4. Spread the eggs evenly with a wooden spatula and cook for about 2-3 min.
5. Using a spatula, ease around the edges and slide to a Servings: plate. Add greens and fold it over in half.

NUTRITION Calories 227 Total fat 3g Total carbohydrate 2.3 g Protein 20g

## EGG AND AVOCADO TOAST

Preparation Time:5 minutes

Cooking Time: 5 minutes

Servings: 2-3

### INGREDIENTS:

- 1 slice whole-grain bread
- 1 teaspoon Dijon mustard
- ¼ avocado, peeled, pitted, and sliced
- 1 hard-boiled egg, cut into slices
- 1 tablespoon chopped fresh cilantro
- Freshly ground black pepper (optional)

**DIRECTIONS:**

1. Toast the bread.
2. Spread the mustard over the toast; then top with the avocado slices.
3. Layer the egg slices on top. Sprinkle with cilantro, season with pepper (if using) to taste, and enjoy.

4. POST-OP TIP: Bread can be filling. I suggest waiting until you are at least six months post-op before adding it to your weekly breakfast rotation. Eat slowly, chew well, and stop when you feel full.

**NUTRITION:(4 OUNCES):** Protein: 12g; Calories: 239; Fat: 12g; Carbohydrates: 22g; Fiber: 6g; Total sugar: 3g; Added sugar: 0g; Sodium: 334g

## OPEN-FACE FETA AND BASIL OMELET

Preparation Time:10 minutes

Cooking Time:5 minutes

Servings: 2-3

**INGREDIENTS:**

- 1 large egg
- 2 tablespoons nonfat milk
- 1 tablespoon fresh basil leaves or ½ teaspoon dried basil
- 1 tablespoon chopped scallion
- Freshly ground black pepper
- 1 teaspoon olive oil
- ½ ounce crumbled feta
- 1 small tomato, cut into wedges

**DIRECTIONS:**

1. In a small bowl, whisk the egg with a fork. Add the milk and beat lightly to combine.
2. Add the basil and scallion and season with pepper to taste. Mix well.
3. In a small pan over medium-low heat, heat the oil. Pour the egg mixture into the pan and sprinkle the feta and tomato on top. Cook for 3 to 4 minutes, or until the egg is set with no liquid remaining.
4. Do not stir. Transfer to a plate and enjoy warm.
5. STORAGE TIP: Make extra omelets, cool them, and refrigerate in an airtight container for up to 3 days.

**NUTRITION:(21/2 OUNCES):** Protein: 10g; Calories: 174; Fat: 13g; Carbohydrates: 6g; Fiber: 1g; Total sugar: 5g; Added sugar: 0g; Sodium: 234mg

## LOX, EGG WHITE, AND AVOCADO SCRAMBLE

Preparation Time:10 minutes

Cooking Time:5 minutes

Servings: 2-3

**INGREDIENTS:**

- 1 teaspoon olive oil
- 2 large egg whites
- Freshly ground black pepper
- 2 ounces lox
- 1½ teaspoons capers, drained and rinsed
- 1½ teaspoons chopped red onion
- 1/8 avocado, peeled, pitted, and cut into slices

**DIRECTIONS:**

1. In a small skillet over low heat, heat the oil. Add the egg whites and cook for 2 to 3 minutes, stirring occasionally, or until no liquid remains. Season with pepper to taste. Spoon the cooked eggs onto a plate.
2. Top with the lox, capers, red onion, and avocado. Enjoy immediately.

**NUTRITION:(4 OUNCES):** Protein: 17g; Calories: 167; Fat: 10g; Carbohydrates: 2g; Fiber: 1g; Total sugar: 1g; Added sugar: 0g; Sodium: 1334mg

## RICOTTA AND SPINACH FRITTATA

Preparation Time:10 minutes

Cooking Time:15 minutes

Servings: 2-3

**INGREDIENTS:**

- 1½ teaspoons olive oil
- 1 tablespoon diced onion
- 1 tablespoon diced mushroom
- ¼ cup fresh spinach
- 1 large egg
- 2 tablespoons part-skim ricotta
- Salt
- Freshly ground black pepper

**DIRECTIONS:**

1. In a small skillet over medium-low heat, heat the oil. Add the onion and sauté for 5 to 7 minutes until golden brown.
2. Add the mushroom and spinach to the skillet. Cook for about 5 minutes until the mushroom is soft and the spinach wilts.
3. In a small bowl, whisk the egg with a fork until smooth.
4. Add the ricotta to the skillet and pour the egg over the top. Season with salt and pepper to taste.

5. Cook for 3 to 4 minutes, without stirring, or until the egg is firm. Serve warm and enjoy.
6. STORAGE TIP: Let the frittata cool completely; then refrigerate in an airtight container for up to 3 days.

**NUTRITION:(4½ OUNCES):** Protein: 10g; Calories: 177; Fat: 14g; Carbohydrates: 3g; Fiber: <1g; Total sugar: 1g; Added sugar: 0g; Sodium: 92mg

# HEARTY WHOLE-GRAIN BREAKFAST BURRITO

Preparation Time:10 minutes

Cooking Time:10 minutes

Servings: 2-3

**INGREDIENTS:**

- ½ teaspoon olive oil or olive oil spray
- 1 large egg
- ¼ cup fat-free refried beans
- 1 tablespoon shredded low-fat Cheddar cheese
- 1 medium (8-inch) whole-grain tortilla
- 1/8 avocado, peeled, pitted, and diced
- ¼ cup fresh spinach
- Salsa, for serving (optional)

**DIRECTIONS:**

1. In a small skillet over medium-low heat, heat the oil.

2. Crack the egg into the skillet and cook, scrambling it with a spatula, for 1 to 2 minutes, or until the egg is almost cooked.
3. Add the beans and cook for 2 to 3 minutes to warm.
4. Add the Cheddar cheese, mix well, and cook for 1 to 2 minutes more until the cheese melts.
5. Warm the tortilla on a plate in the microwave on high power for about 1 minute.
6. Spoon the eggs, beans, and cheese onto the warm tortilla. Top with avocado, spinach, and salsa (if using). Fold into a burrito and enjoy.

**STORAGE TIP:** Double or triple the burrito filling and, once cool, refrigerate in an airtight container for up to 3 days. When ready to eat, warm a tortilla as you reheat the filling; then spoon the filling into the tortilla and top with spinach, avocado, and salsa.

**NUTRITION:**(5½ ounces): Protein: 14g; Calories: 256; Fat: 12g; Carbohydrates: 23g; Fiber: 14g; Total sugar: 1g; Added sugar: 0g; Sodium: 525mg

## TURKEY, CHEESE, AND HASH BROWN MINI-BAKE

Preparation Time:10 minutes

Cooking Time:20 minutes

Servings: 2-3

### INGREDIENTS:

- Olive oil spray
- 4 ounces lean ground turkey
- Salt
- Freshly ground black pepper
- Onion powder, for seasoning
- Garlic powder, for seasoning
- 1 tablespoon canned diced green chiles
- ½ cup frozen hash browns
- 2 tablespoons shredded low-fat Cheddar cheese

### DIRECTIONS:

1. Preheat the oven 425°F.
2. Coat 2 (6-ounce) ramekins with olive oil spray.
3. Evenly divide the ground turkey between the prepared ramekins. Season with salt, pepper, onion powder, and garlic powder to taste. Top each with 11/2 teaspoons of green chiles and ¼ cup of hash browns.
4. Bake for 10 to 15 minutes, or until the turkey is fully cooked with no pink remaining.
5. Top each with 1 tablespoon of Cheddar cheese and bake for 3 to 5 minutes more until the cheese melts. Enjoy warm.

**COOKING TIP:** Double or triple this recipe and cook it in a casserole dish or muffin tin for extra portions you can reheat and eat throughout the week.

**NUTRITION:(1 RAMEKIN; 4 OUNCES):** Protein: 18g; Calories: 179; Fat: 7g; Carbohydrates: 10g; Fiber: 1g; Total sugar: 1g; Added sugar: 0g; Sodium: 154g

## SMOOTHIE BOWL WITH GREEK YOGURT AND FRESH BERRIES

Preparation Time:5 Minutes

Cooking Time:5 Minutes

Servings: 2-3

### INGREDIENTS:

- ¾ cup unsweetened vanilla almond milk or low-fat milk
- ¼ cup low-fat plain Greek yogurt
- 1/3 cup (1 handful) fresh spinach
- ½ scoop (1/8 cup) plain or vanilla protein powder
- ¼ cup frozen mixed berries
- ¼ cup fresh raspberries
- ¼ cup fresh blueberries
- 1 tablespoon sliced, slivered almonds
- 1 teaspoon chia seeds
- Post-Op Servings
- 1 bowl

### DIRECTIONS:

1. In a blender, combine the milk, yogurt, spinach, protein powder, and frozen berries. Blend on high speed for 3 to 4 minutes, until the powder is well dissolved and no longer visible.
2. Pour the smoothie into small bowl.
3. Decorate the smoothie with the fresh raspberries, blueberries, almonds, and chia seeds.
4. Serve with a spoon and enjoy!

**Serving tip:** You can make this smoothie bowl with a variety of other fruits and toppings to change it up. Try a mango-pineapple version. Top with unsweetened, flaked coconut and use coconut milk in the smoothie base for a more tropical vibe.

**NUTRITION:(1 BOWL):** Calories: 255; Total fat: 10 g; Protein: 20g; Carbs: 21g; Fiber: 8g; Sugar: 10g; Sodium: 262mg

## HIGH-PROTEIN PANCAKES

Preparation Time:5 Minutes

Cooking Time:5 Minutes

Servings: 2-3

### INGREDIENTS:

- 3 eggs
- 1 cup low-fat cottage cheese
- 1/3 cup whole-wheat pastry flour
- 1½ tablespoons coconut oil, melted
- Nonstick cooking spray
- Post-Op Servings
- ½ pancake
- 1 to 2 pancakes

### DIRECTIONS:

1. In large bowl, lightly whisk the eggs.
2. Whisk in the cottage cheese, flour, and coconut oil just until combined.
3. Heat a large skillet or griddle over medium heat, and lightly coat with the cooking spray.
4. Using a measuring cup, pour 1/3 cup of batter into the skillet for each pancake. Cook for 2 to 3 minutes, or until bubbles appear across the surface of each pancake. Flip over the pancakes and cook for 1 to 2

minutes on the other side, or until golden brown.

5. Serve immediately.

**Serving tip:** Top these pancakes with fresh berries and plain yogurt, unsweetened applesauce, or sugar-free syrup. You can even try them with natural peanut butter and bananas on a general diet.

**NUTRITION: (1 PANCAKE):** Calories: 182; Total fat: 10g; Protein: 12g; Carbs: 10g; Fiber: 3g; Sugar: 1g; Sodium: 68mg

## BAKED EGG, PARM, AND SPINACH CUP

Preparation Time:10 minutes

Cooking Time:10 minutes

Servings: 2-3

### INGREDIENTS:

- Nonstick cooking spray
- ¼ cup chopped fresh spinach
- 1 large egg
- 1 tablespoon nonfat milk

- ½ tomato, diced
- 1 tablespoon grated Parmesan cheese
- Freshly ground black pepper

## DIRECTIONS:

1. Preheat the oven to 400°F. Coat a 6-ounce ramekin with cooking spray.
2. Place the spinach in the ramekin; then crack the egg over the top.
3. Add the milk, tomato, and Parmesan cheese. Season with pepper to taste.
4. Bake for 10 minutes, or until set. Enjoy warm.

**STORAGE TIP:** Double or triple the recipe and make several egg cups at once. Let the egg cups cool; then tightly cover with plastic wrap and refrigerate for up 3 days. You can also cook several at once in a muffin tin (for 10 to 15 minutes until set), cool, and then refrigerate each in a sealed plastic zip-top bag for up to 3 days.

**NUTRITION:(1 RAMEKIN; 3 OUNCES):** Protein: 9g; Calories: 112; Fat: 7g; Carbohydrates: 5g; Fiber: 1g; Total sugar: 3g; Added sugar: 0g; Sodium: 183g

## PUMPKIN MUFFINS WITH WALNUTS AND ZUCCHINI

Preparation Time:10 Minutes

Cooking Time:25 Minutes

Servings: 2-3

### INGREDIENTS:

- Nonstick cooking spray or baking liners
- 2 cups old-fashioned oats
- 1¾ cups whole-wheat pastry flour
- ¼ cup ground flaxseed
- 2 tablespoons baking powder
- 1 teaspoon baking soda
- 1 teaspoon ground cinnamon
- ¼ teaspoon ground nutmeg
- ¼ teaspoon ground ginger
- ¼ teaspoon ground allspice
- 2 cups shredded zucchini
- 1 cup canned pumpkin or fresh pumpkin puree
- 1 cup low-fat milk
- 4 eggs, lightly beaten
- ¼ cup unsweetened applesauce
- 1 teaspoon liquid stevia
- ½ cup chopped walnuts
- Post-Op Servings
- 1 muffin

### DIRECTIONS:

1. Preheat the oven to 375°F. Prepare two muffin tins by coating the cups with the cooking spray, or use baking liners.
2. In large bowl, mix together the oats, flour, flaxseed, baking powder, baking soda, cinnamon, nutmeg, ginger, and allspice.
3. In a separate medium bowl mix together the zucchini, pumpkin, milk, eggs, applesauce, and stevia.
4. Add the wet ingredients to the dry and stir to combine. Gently stir in the walnuts.
5. Fill the cups of the muffin tins about half full with the batter.
6. Bake until the muffins are done, when a toothpick inserted in the center comes out clean, about 25 minutes.
7. Let the muffins cool for 5 minutes before removing them from the tins. Place on a baking rack to finish cooling.
8. Wrap leftover muffins in plastic wrap and freeze. Reheat frozen muffins in the microwave for about 20 seconds.

**NUTRITION:(1 MUFFIN):** Calories: 128; Total fat: 5g; Protein: 5g; Carbs: 18g; Fiber: 3g; Sugar: 1g; Sodium: 86mg

## HARD-BOILED EGGS AND AVOCADO ON TOAST

Preparation Time:10 Minutes

Cooking Time:10 Minutes

Servings: 2-3

### INGREDIENTS:

- 4 eggs
- 4 slices sprouted whole-wheat bread, such as Angelic Bakehouse Sprouted Grain
- 1 medium avocado
- 1 teaspoon hot sauce
- Freshly ground black pepper
- Post-Op Servings
- 1 toast

### DIRECTIONS:

1. Bring a large pot of water to a rapid boil over high heat.
2. Carefully add the eggs to the boiling water using a spoon, and set a timer for 10 minutes.
3. Immediately transfer the eggs from the boiling water to a strainer, and run cold water over the eggs to stop the cooking process.
4. Once the eggs are cool enough to handle, peel them and slice lengthwise into fourths.
5. Toast the bread.
6. While the bread toasts, mash the avocado with a fork in a small bowl and mix in the hot sauce.
7. Spread the avocado mash evenly across each toast. Top each toast slice with 4 egg slices and season with the black pepper.

**INGREDIENT TIP:** Avocado is rich in healthy fat, but also loaded with calories, so portion control is key. Store the pit with any unused portion of avocado, squeeze a teaspoon of lemon juice over the leftovers, and place in an airtight container or wrap in plastic wrap to prevent browning.

**NUTRITION:(1 TOAST): CALORIES:** 191; Total fat: 10g; Protein: 10g; Carbs: 15g; Fiber: 5g; Sugar: 1g; Sodium: 214mg

## EGGS WITH CAULIFLOWER

Preparation Time:5 Minutes

Cooking Time:5 Minutes

Servings: 2-3

### INGREDIENTS:

- ½ (10-ounce) bag of frozen cauliflower florets
- 4 thin slices (nitrate-free) deli ham
- Nonstick cooking spray
- 2 large eggs
- Post-Op Servings
- ½ recipe

### DIRECTIONS:

1. Place the cauliflower with 2 tablespoons water in a microwave-safe bowl or steamer. Cover and cook on high for 4 minutes, or until tender. During the last 30 seconds, add the ham to heat it thoroughly. Drain off any water after cooking.
2. Coat a small skillet with the cooking spray and place it over medium-high heat. Crack two eggs into a small dish and set aside.
3. When the skillet is hot, carefully add the eggs. Reduce the heat to medium-low.

Jiggle the pan slightly and then allow eggs to cook for 2 to 3 minutes, or until the whites turn opaque and the yolk starts to cook but is still soft in the center. If necessary, use a rubber spatula to adjust the egg slightly to prevent it from sticking. Place the cauliflower on a plate and the ham on top of the cauliflower. Add the eggs, allowing the yolk to spill over the entire dish. Eat immediately.

**SERVING TIP:** If tolerated, this is also excellent served over steamed asparagus tips instead of cauliflower.

**NUTRITION:(½ RECIPE):** Calories: 109; Total fat: 6g; Protein: 11g; Carbs: 4g; Fiber: 2g; Sugar: 1g;   Sodium: 378mg

## SOUTHWESTERN SCRAMBLED EGG BURRITOS

Preparation Time:10 Minutes

Cooking Time:10 Minutes

Servings: 2-3

### INGREDIENTS:

- 12 eggs
- ¼ cup low-fat milk
- 1 teaspoon extra-virgin olive oil
- ½ onion, chopped
- 1 red bell pepper, diced
- 1 green bell pepper, diced
- 1 (15-ounce) can black beans, drained and rinsed
- 8 (7- to 8-inch) whole-wheat tortillas, such as La Tortilla Factory low-carb tortillas
- 1 cup salsa, for serving
- Post-Op Servings
- Burrito filling (no tortilla)
- ½ to 1 burrito

### DIRECTIONS:

1. In a large bowl, whisk together the eggs and milk. Set aside.
2. In a large skillet over medium-high heat, heat the olive oil and add the onion and bell peppers. Sauté for 2 to 3 minutes, or until tender. Add the beans and stir to combine.
3. Add the egg mixture. Reduce the heat to medium-low and stir gently and constantly with a rubber spatula for 5 minutes, until the eggs are fluffy and cooked through.
4. Divide the scrambled egg mixture among the tortillas. Fold over the bottom end of the tortilla, fold in the sides, and roll tightly to close.
5. Serve immediately with the salsa, or place each burrito in a zip-top bag and refrigerate for up to 1 week. To eat, reheat each burrito in the microwave for 60 to 90 seconds. These will also keep well in the freezer for up to 1 month.

**SERVING TIP:** To get more vegetables into your breakfast, buy a bag of frozen California-blend mixed vegetables. Heat some in a skillet with extra-virgin olive oil, add eggs, and—voilà! —a quick veggie-packed egg burrito.

**NUTRITION:(1 BURRITO):** Calories: 250; Total fat: 10g; Protein: 19g; Carbs: 28g; Fiber: 13g; Sugar: 1g; Sodium: 546mg

## FARMER'S EGG CASSEROLE WITH BROCCOLI, MUSHROOM, AND ONIONS

Preparation Time:10 Minutes

Cooking Time:40 Minutes

Servings: 2-3

### INGREDIENTS:

- Nonstick cooking spray
- 2 teaspoons extra-virgin olive oil
- 1 onion, diced
- ½ cup chopped mushrooms
- 2 cups roughly chopped broccoli florets
- 12 eggs
- 2 tablespoons low-fat milk
- ½ teaspoon dried oregano
- ½ teaspoon dried basil
- ¼ teaspoon dried thyme
- 1 cup chopped or shredded cooked poultry breast, such as leftover turkey or chicken, canned chicken breast, or turkey lunch meat (nitrate-free)
- 1 cup shredded Swiss cheese
- ¼ cup shredded Parmigiano-Reggiano cheese
- Post-Op Servings
- 1 (3-by-4-inch) piece

### DIRECTIONS:

1. Preheat the oven to 350°F. Spray a 9-by-13-inch baking dish with the cooking spray.
2. In a large skillet over medium heat, add the olive oil. When the oil is hot, add the onion and sauté for 1 to 2 minutes, or until tender. Add the mushrooms and cook for an additional 2 to 3 minutes, or until tender.
3. In a steamer or microwave-safe bowl, place the broccoli florets and 2 tablespoons water. Cover and microwave/steam for about 4 minutes or just until tender. Drain off any liquid and set aside.
4. In a large bowl, whisk together the eggs, milk, oregano, basil, and thyme.
5. Add the cooked vegetables, poultry, and Swiss cheese to the egg mixture and stir to combine.
6. Pour the mixture into the baking dish and sprinkle the Parmigiano-Reggiano cheese over the top.
7. Bake for 35 to 40 minutes, or until lightly browned. Let the casserole rest for 5 minutes before serving.
8. Store leftovers in the refrigerator for up to 1 week. Reheat before eating.

**SERVING TIP:** Customize this egg casserole with whatever is in your pantry. Try to use vegetables that are in season. Try a Southwest version with chopped bell peppers and topped with fresh salsa. Make a spinach-artichoke bake with canned artichoke hearts. Egg casseroles can be a great way to get plenty of vegetables and a variety of proteins, so shake it up to keep it interesting.

**NUTRITION:(1 [3-BY-4-INCH] PIECE):** Calories: 147; Total fat: 10g; Protein: 12g; Carbs: 2g; Fiber: 1g; Sugar: 0g; Sodium: 193mg

## CHERRY AVOCADO SMOOTHIE

Preparation Time: 5 minutes

Cooking Time: 2 minutes

Servings: 2-3

### INGREDIENTS:

- ½ ripe avocado, chopped
- 1 cup fresh cherries
- 1 cup coconut water, sugar-free
- 1 whole lime

### DIRECTIONS:

1. Peel the avocado and cut in half. Remove the pit and chop into bite-sized pieces. Reserve the rest in the refrigerator. Set aside.
2. Rinse the cherries under cold running water using a large colander. Cut each in half and remove the pits. Set aside.
3. Peel the lime and cut in half. Set aside.
4. Now, combine avocado, cherries, coconut water, and lime in a blender. Pulse to combine and transfer to a serving glass.
5. Add few ice cubes and refrigerate for 10 minutes before serving.

**NUTRITION:** Net carbs 17 g Fiber 3.8 g Fats 6.8 g Sugar 3 g Calories 128

# CHAPTER 7. SIDES AND SNACKS

## . SIMPLY VANILLA FROZEN GREEK YOGURT

Preparation Time: 5 minutes + 8 hours to freeze

Cooking Time: 0 minutes

Servings: 2-3

**INGREDIENTS:**

- 4 cups nonfat plain Greek yogurt
- 4 tablespoons vanilla whey protein powder
- 4 tablespoons vanilla extract
- 4 teaspoons stevia or no-calorie sweetener

**DIRECTIONS:**

1. In a large bowl or loaf pan, combine the yogurt, protein powder, vanilla extract, and stevia.
2. Cover and freeze overnight or for at least 8 hours.
3. About an hour before serving, set in the refrigerator to thaw slightly. Serve and enjoy.

**NUTRITION: PER SERVING (1 CUP):** Calories: 183; Protein: 28g; Fat: 1g; Carbohydrates: 12g; Fiber: 1g; Sugar: 8g; Sodium: 96mg

## GREEK CHOP-CHOP SALAD

Preparation Time: 15 minutes

Cooking Time: 0 minutes

Servings: 4-5

**INGREDIENTS:**

- 1 medium English cucumber, chopped (2 cups)
- 1 cup halved cherry tomatoes
- 1 red bell pepper, seeded and diced
- ½ red onion, diced
- ½ cup pitted Kalamata olives, roughly chopped
- 1 cup crumbled feta cheese
- ½ cup balsamic dressing

**DIRECTIONS:**

1. In a large bowl, toss the cucumber, tomatoes, bell pepper, onion, olives, and cheese with the dressing, and serve.

**NUTRITION:** Calories: 173; Total fat: 13g; Protein: 4g; Carbohydrates: 10g; Fiber: 1g; Sugar: 4g; Sodium: 883mg.

## CHIA CHOCOLATE PUDDING

Preparation Time: 5 minutes + 2-8 hours to chill

Cooking Time: 0 minutes

Servings: 2-3

**INGREDIENTS:**

- ½ cup unsweetened almond milk
- ½ cup nonfat plain Greek yogurt
- 2 tablespoons chia seeds
- 1 tablespoon vanilla whey protein
- 1 teaspoon unsweetened cocoa powder
- ½ teaspoon stevia or no-calorie sweetener

**DIRECTIONS:**

1. In a canning jar, combine the almond milk, yogurt, chia seeds, whey protein, cocoa powder, and stevia.
2. Seal with lid and let sit in refrigerator overnight.
3. Enjoy straight from the jar, or in a separate bowl if you are consuming a smaller serving.

**NUTRITION:** Calories: 257; Protein: 25g; Fat: 12g; Carbohydrates: 21g; Fiber: 11g; Sugar: 5g; Sodium: 122mg

## MASHED CAULIFLOWER

Preparation Time: 10 minutes

Cooking Time: 5 minutes

Servings: 2-3

### INGREDIENTS:

- 1 large head cauliflower
- ¼ cup water
- 1/3 cup low-fat buttermilk
- 1 tablespoon minced garlic
- 1 tablespoon extra-virgin olive oil

### DIRECTIONS:

1. Break the cauliflower into small florets. Place in a large microwave-safe bowl with the water. Cover and microwave for about 5 minutes, or until the cauliflower is soft. Drain the water from the bowl.
2. In a blender or food processor, puree the buttermilk, cauliflower, garlic, and olive oil on medium speed until the cauliflower is smooth and creamy.
3. Serve immediately.

**NUTRITION:** Calories: 62; Total fat: 2g; Protein: 3g; Carbs: 8g; Fiber: 3g; Sugar: 3g; Sodium: 54mg

## PICKLE ROLL-UPS

Preparation Time: 20 minutes

Cooking Time: 0 minutes

Servings: 2-3

### INGREDIENTS:

- ¼ pound deli ham (nitrate-free), thinly sliced (about 8 slices)
- 8 ounces Neufchâtel cheese, at room temperature
- 1 teaspoon dried dill
- 1 teaspoon onion powder
- 8 whole kosher dill pickle spears

### DIRECTIONS:

1. Get a large cutting board or clean counter space to assemble your roll-ups.
2. Lay the ham slices on the work surface and carefully spread on the Neufchâtel cheese.
3. Season each lightly with the dill and onion powder.
4. Place an entire pickle on an end of the ham and carefully roll.
5. Slice each pickle roll-up into mini rounds about ½- to 1-inch wide.
6. Skew each with a toothpick for easier serving.

**NUTRITION:** Calories: 86; Total fat: 7g; Protein: 4g; Carbs: 4g; Fiber: 0 g; Sugar: 2g; Sodium: 540mg

## BAKED ZUCCHINI FRIES

Preparation Time: 15 minutes

Cooking Time: 15 minutes

Servings: 2-3

### INGREDIENTS:

- 3 large zucchinis
- 2 large eggs
- 1 cup whole-wheat bread crumbs
- ¼ cup shredded Parmigiano-Reggiano cheese
- 1 teaspoon garlic powder
- 1 teaspoon onion powder

### DIRECTIONS:

1. Preheat the oven to 425°F. Line a large rimmed baking sheet with aluminum foil.
2. Halve each zucchini lengthwise and continue slicing each piece into fries about ½ inch in diameter. You will have about 8 strips per zucchini.
3. In a small bowl, crack the eggs and beat lightly.

4. In a medium bowl, combine the bread crumbs, Parmigiano-Reggiano cheese, garlic powder, and onion powder.
5. One by one, dip each zucchini strip into the egg, then roll it in the bread crumb mixture. Place on the prepared baking sheet.

6. Roast for 30 minutes, stirring the fries halfway through. Zucchini fries are done when brown and crispy.
7. Serve immediately.

**NUTRITION:** Calories: 89; Total fat: 3g; Protein: 5g; Carbs: 10g; Fiber: 1g; Sugar: 3g; Sodium: 179mg

## ITALIAN EGGPLANT PIZZAS

Preparation Time: 15 minutes

Cooking Time: 15 minutes

Servings: 2-3

**INGREDIENTS:**

- 1 large eggplant, cut into ¼- to ½-inch rounds
- 1 tablespoon salt
- 1 tablespoon extra-virgin olive oil
- 2 teaspoons minced garlic
- ½ teaspoon dried oregano
- 1 cup Marinara Sauce with Italian Herbs
- 1 cup fresh basil leaves
- 1 cup shredded part-skim Mozzarella cheese
- ¼ cup shredded Parmigiano-Reggiano cheese

**DIRECTIONS:**

1. Preheat the oven to 425°F. Line a large rimmed baking sheet with aluminum foil.
2. Put the eggplant rounds on paper towels and sprinkle them with the salt. Let them sit for 10 to 15 minutes to help release some of the water in the eggplant. Pat dry afterward. It's okay to wipe off some of the salt before baking.
3. In a small bowl, mix together the olive oil, garlic, and oregano.
4. Place the eggplant rounds 1-inch apart on the baking sheet. Using a pastry brush, coat each side of the eggplant with the olive oil mixture. Bake the eggplant for 15 minutes.
5. Create pizzas by layering 1 to 2 tablespoons of marinara sauce, 2 basil leaves, about 1 tablespoon of mozzarella cheese, and about ½ tablespoon of Parmigiano-Reggiano cheese on each baked eggplant round.
6. Bake the pizzas for an additional 10 minutes or until the cheese is melted and starting to brown.
7. Serve immediately and enjoy!

**NUTRITION:** Calories: 99; Total fat: 6g; Protein: 5g; Carbs: 7g; Fiber: 2g; Sugar: 4g; Sodium: 500mg

## BLUEBERRY GREEK YOGURT PANCAKES

Preparation Time: 10 minutes

Cooking Time: 8 minutes

Servings: 2-3

**INGREDIENTS:**

- 2 - large eggs
- ¾ - cup plain 2-percent-fat Greek yogurt
- ½ - tablespoons honey, divided
- ½ - teaspoon vanilla extract
- ½ - cup whole wheat flour
- 1 - teaspoon baking powder
- 1 - pinch salt
- ¼ - teaspoon cinnamon
- 1 - cup fresh (or frozen, thawed) blueberries
- 2 - tablespoons natural peanut butter, divided

**DIRECTIONS:**

1. In a bowl, beat eggs. Blend in yogurt, 2 tbsp. nectar, and vanilla. In another bowl, mix together flour, heating powder, salt, and cinnamon. Blend in 1/2 cup blueberries.

2. In an enormous nonstick skillet covered with a cooking splash over medium-low heat, drop a stacking 1/4 cup hitter for every flapjack. Cook until underside is dark-colored and air pockets structure on top, around 3 minutes. Flip and cook around 3 minutes more.

3. Top each presenting with 1/2 tbsp. nectar, 1 tbsp. nutty spread, and 1/4 cup blueberries.

**NUTRITION:** Calories: 6; Carbs: 54g; Sugar: 25g; Protein: 23g

## EGG WHITE PORRIDGE WITH STRAWBERRIES AND PEANUT BUTTER

Preparation Time: 2 minutes

Cooking Time: 5 minutes

Servings: 2-3

### INGREDIENTS:

- ½ - cup porridge
- ½ - cup unsweetened almond milk
- 6 - large fresh (or frozen, thawed) strawberries, cored and chopped
- 2 - teaspoons honey
- ½ - teaspoon vanilla extract
- 1 - pinch salt
- 1/3 - cup liquid egg whites
- 1 - tablespoon peanut butter

### DIRECTIONS:

1. In a little pot, heat porridge, 2 cup almond milk, 1/3 cup water, strawberries, nectar, vanilla, and salt. Heat to the point of boiling, at that point decrease to stew and cook, blending once in a while, until the blend is thick, 5 to 7minutes. Expel from warm.

2. In a bowl, whisk egg whites until somewhat bubbly. Add cooked cereal to egg whites a spoonful at once, rushing between every option, until oats are completely joined.

3. Pour blend once more into the pot and cook over low heat, mixing always, until oats are thick, 2 to minutes. Be mindful so as not to turn the warmth excessively high so eggs don't scramble.

4. Top cereal with nutty spread.

**NUTRITION:** Calories 412; carbs g; sugar 17g; protein 20g

# CHAPTER 8. FISH AND SEAFOOD

## CARAMELIZED SALMON FILLET

Preparation Time: 5 minutes

Cooking Time: 25 minutes

Servings: 2-3

### INGREDIENTS:

- 2 salmon fillets
- 60g cane sugar
- 4 tbsp soy sauce
- 50g sesame seeds
- Unlimited Ginger

### DIRECTIONS:

1. Preheat the air fryer at 1800C for 5 minutes.
2. Put the sugar and soy sauce in the basket.
3. Cook everything for 5 minutes.
4. In the meantime, wash the fish well, pass it through sesame to cover it completely and place it inside the tank and add the fresh ginger.
5. Cook for 12 minutes.
6. Turn the fish over and finish cooking for another 8 minutes.

**NUTRITION:** Calories 569 Fat 14.9 g Carbohydrates 40 g Sugars 27.6 g Protein 66.9 g Cholesterol 165.3 mg

## SALMON BUTTER CRUMBED

Preparation Time: 5-10 min.

Cooking Time: 10 min.

Servings: 2-3

### INGREDIENTS:

- 1 tablespoon thyme, chopped
- 2 garlic cloves, minced
- 1 1/2 cups soft bread crumbs
- 2 tablespoons minced parsley
- 1 teaspoon grated lemon zest
- 1/2 teaspoon salt
- 1/4 teaspoon paprika
- 1 tablespoon butter, melted
- 1/4 teaspoon lemon-pepper seasoning
- 2 salmon fillets (6 ounces each)

### DIRECTIONS:

1. In a mixing bowl, add bread crumbs, fresh parsley thyme, garlic, lemon zest, salt, lemon-pepper seasoning, and paprika. Combine to mix well with each other.
2. Place Instant Pot over kitchen platform. Place Air Fryer Lid on top. Press Air Fry, set the temperature to 375°F and set the timer to 5 minutes to preheat. Press "Start" and allow it to preheat for 5 minutes.
3. Take Air Fryer Basket, grease it with some cooking spray. In the basket, add salmon fillets skin side down and top with the crumb mixture.
4. Place the basket in the inner pot of Instant Pot, close Air Fryer Lid on top.

5. Press the "Bake" setting. Set temperature to 390°F and set the timer to 10 minutes. Press "Start."
6. Open Air Fryer Lid after cooking time is over. Serve warm.

**NUTRITION:** Calories: 308 Fat: 17g Saturated Fat: 2.5g Trans Fat: 0g Carbohydrates: 11.5g Fiber: 1g Sodium: 347mg Protein: 9g

## CAJUN SHRIMP

Preparation Time: 5 minutes

Cooking Time: 5 minutes

Servings: 2-3

**INGREDIENTS:**

- Tiger shrimp (16-20/1.25 lb.)
- Olive oil (1 tbsp.)
- Old Bay seasoning (.5 tsp.)
- Smoked paprika (.25 tsp.)
- Cayenne pepper (.25 tsp.)

**DIRECTIONS:**

1. Set the Air Fryer at 390° Fahrenheit.
2. Cover the shrimp using the oil and spices.
3. Toss them into the Air Fryer basket and set the timer for five minutes.
4. Serve with your favorite side dish.

**NUTRITION:** Calories 356; Fat 18g; Carbohydrates 5 g; Protein 34g;

## VEGETABLE EGG HALIBUT

Preparation Time: 5-10 min.

Cooking Time: 15 min.

Servings: 3-4

**INGREDIENTS:**

- 2 pounds mixed vegetables
- 4 cups torn lettuce leaves
- 1 cup cherry tomatoes, halved
- 1 ½ pounds halibut fillets
- Black pepper (ground) and salt to taste
- 2 tablespoons olive oil
- 4 large hard-boiled eggs, sliced

**DIRECTIONS:**

1. Rub the halibut with salt and black pepper. Coat fish with oil.
2. Place Instant Pot over kitchen platform. Place Air Fryer Lid on top. Press Air Fry, set the temperature to 375°F and set the timer to 5 minutes to preheat. Press "Start" and allow it to preheat for 5 minutes.
3. Take Air Fryer Basket, grease it with some cooking spray. In the basket, add fish and arrange vegetables around.
4. Place the basket in the inner pot of Instant Pot, close Air Fryer Lid on top.
5. Press the "Air Fry" setting. Set temperature to 375°F and set the timer to 15 minutes. Press "Start." Stir the mixture halfway down.
6. Open Air Fryer Lid after cooking time is over. Serve warm in a bowl mixed with eggs, lettuce, and tomatoes.

**NUTRITION:** Calories: 336 Fat: 11g Saturated Fat: 3g Trans Fat: 0g Carbohydrates: 16g Fiber: 2g Sodium: 658mg Protein: 20.5g

## DEEP FRIED PRAWNS

Preparation Time: 15 minutes

Cooking Time: 10 minutes

Servings: 2-3

**INGREDIENTS:**

- 12 prawns
- 2 eggs
- Flour to taste
- Breadcrumbs
- 1 tsp oil

**DIRECTIONS:**

1. Remove the head of the prawns and shell carefully.
2. Pass the prawns first in the flour, then in the beaten egg and then in the breadcrumbs.
3. Preheat the air fryer for 1 minute at 1500C.

4. Add the prawns and cook for 4 minutes. If the prawns are large, it will be necessary to cook 6 at a time.
5. Turn the prawns and cook for another 4 minutes.
6. They should be served with a yogurt or mayonnaise sauce.

**NUTRITION:** Calories 2385.1 Fat 23 Carbohydrates 52.3g Sugar 0.1g Protein 21.4g

## SALMON WITH PISTACHIO BARK

Preparation Time: 10 minutes

Cooking Time: 15 minutes

Servings: 2-3

**INGREDIENTS:**

- 600 g salmon fillet
- 50g pistachios
- Salt to taste

**DIRECTIONS:**

1. Put the parchment paper on the bottom of the air fryer basket and place the salmon fillet in it (it can be cooked whole or already divided into four portions).
2. Cut the pistachios in thick pieces; grease the top of the fish, salt (little because the pistachios are already salted) and cover everything with the pistachios.
3. Set the air fryer to 1800C and simmer for 25 minutes.

**NUTRITION:** Calories 371.7 Fat 21.8 g Carbohydrate 9.4 g Sugars 2.2g Protein 34.7 g Cholesterol 80.5 mg

## GRILLED SARDINES

Preparation Time: 5 minutes

Cooking Time: 10 minutes

Servings: 2-3

**INGREDIENTS:**

- 5 sardines
- Herbs of Provence

**DIRECTIONS:**

1. Preheat the air fryer to 1600C.
2. Spray the basket and place your sardines in the basket of your fryer.
3. Set the timer for 14 minutes. After 7 minutes, remember to turn the sardines so that they are roasted on both sides.

**NUTRITION:** Calories 189g Fat 10g Carbohydrates 0g Sugars 0g Protein 22g Cholesterol 128mg

## RANGOON CRAB DIP

Preparation Time: 10 minutes

Cooking Time: 16 minutes

Servings: 2-3

**INGREDIENTS:**

- 2 cups crab meat
- 1 cup mozzarella cheese, shredded
- 1/2 tsp garlic powder
- 1/4 cup pimentos, drained and diced
- 1/4 tsp stevia
- 1/2 lemon juice
- 2 tsp coconut amino
- 2 tsp mayonnaise
- 8 oz cream cheese, softened
- 1 tbsp green onion
- 1/4 tsp pepper
- Salt

**DIRECTIONS:**

1. Preheat the air fryer to 325 F.
2. Add all ingredients except half mozzarella cheese into the large bowl and mix until well combined.
3. Transfer bowl mixture into the air fryer baking dish and sprinkle with remaining mozzarella cheese.
4. Place into the air fryer and cook for 16 minutes.
5. Serve and enjoy.

**NUTRITION:** Calories 141 Fat 11.5 g Carbohydrates 4.9 g Sugar 1.7 g Protein 4.9 g Cholesterol 38 mg

## PERFECT CRAB DIP

Preparation Time: 5 minutes

Cooking Time: 7 minutes

Servings: 2-3

### INGREDIENTS:

- 1 cup crabmeat
- 2 tbsp parsley, chopped
- 2 tbsp fresh lemon juice
- 2 tbsp hot sauce
- 1/2 cup green onion, sliced
- 2 cups cheese, grated
- 1/4 cup mayonnaise
- 1/4 tsp pepper
- 1/2 tsp salt

### DIRECTIONS:

1. In a 6-inch dish, mix together crabmeat, hot sauce, cheese, mayo, pepper, and salt.
2. Place dish in air fryer basket and cook dip at 400 F for 7 minutes.
3. Remove dish from air fryer.
4. Drizzle dip with lemon juice and garnish with parsley.
5. Serve and enjoy.

**NUTRITION:** Calories 313 Fat 23.9 g Carbohydrates 8.8 g Sugar 3.1 g Protein 16.2 g Cholesterol 67 mg

## CRAB MUSHROOMS

Preparation Time: 10 minutes

Cooking Time: 8 minutes

Servings: 2-3

### INGREDIENTS:

- 16 mushrooms, clean and chop stems
- 1/4 tsp chili powder
- 1/4 tsp onion powder
- 1/4 cup mozzarella cheese, shredded
- 2 oz crab meat, chopped
- 8 oz cream cheese, softened
- 2 tsp garlic, minced
- 1/4 tsp pepper

### DIRECTIONS:

1. In a mixing bowl, mix together stems, chili powder, onion powder, pepper, cheese, crabmeat, cream cheese, and garlic until well combined.
2. Stuff mushrooms with bowl mixture and place into the air fryer basket.
3. Cook mushrooms at 370 F for 8 minutes.
4. Serve and enjoy.

**NUTRITION:** Calories 59 Fat 5.1 g Carbohydrates 1.2 g Sugar 0.4 g Protein 2.2 g Cholesterol 18 mg

## TUNA NOODLE-LESS CASSEROLE

Preparation Time: 15 minutes

Cooking Time: 40 minutes

Servings: 2-3-2

### INGREDIENTS:

- Nonstick cooking spray
- 1 medium red onion, chopped

- 1 red bell pepper, chopped
- 1½ cups diced tomato
- 3 cups fresh green beans
- 1/3 cup olive oil-based mayonnaise
- 1 (14.5-ounce) can condensed cream of mushroom soup
- ½ cup low-fat milk
- 1 cup shredded Cheddar cheese
- ½ teaspoon freshly ground black pepper
- 8 (5-ounce) cans water-packed albacore tuna, drained

## DIRECTIONS:

1. Preheat the oven to 425°F.
2. Coat a large skillet with the cooking spray and place it over medium heat. Add the onion, red bell pepper, and tomatoes and sauté for about 5 minutes, or until the vegetables are tender and the tomatoes start to soften. Remove the skillet from the heat and set aside.
3. Cut off the stem ends of the green beans, and snap them into 3- to 4-inch pieces.
4. Fill a large saucepot 1/3 full with water, and place a steamer basket inside. Place the pot over high heat, and bring the water to a boil.
5. Add the green beans to the steamer basket, cover the pot, and reduce the heat to medium. Steam the green beans for 5 minutes. Immediately remove them from the heat, drain, and set aside.
6. Coat a 9-by-13-inch baking dish with the cooking spray.
7. In a large bowl, mix together the mayonnaise, condensed soup, milk, and cheese. Season the mixture with the black pepper.
8. Add the tuna, green beans, and sautéed vegetables to the bowl, and mix to combine. Pour the mixture into the baking dish.
9. Serve after baking for 30 minutes and brown.

**Cooking tip:** It's easy to shake up this standby recipe. To boost protein and reduce fat, add ½ cup of nonfat cottage cheese and reduce the mayonnaise to 2 tablespoons. Use an immersion blender to puree until smooth. To change the flavor profile, first sauté the diced tomatoes in 1 teaspoon of extra-virgin olive oil for 5 minutes before cooking the rest of the vegetables.

Set the sautéed tomatoes aside and mix them in with the tuna. Then follow the rest of directions to put together the casserole. The tomatoes become almost like sun-dried and help attenuate some of the fishiness of the tuna.

**NUTRITION:** Per Serving (1 cup): Calories: 147; Total fat: 7g; Protein: 15g; Carbs: 6g; Fiber: 2g; Sugar: 2g; Sodium: 318mg

## SLOW-ROASTED PESTO SALMON

Preparation Time: 5 minutes

Cooking Time: 10 minutes

Servings: 2-3

### INGREDIENTS:

- 4 (6-ounce) salmon fillets
- 1 teaspoon extra-virgin olive oil
- 4 tablespoons Perfect Basil Pesto

### DIRECTIONS:

1. Preheat the oven to 275°F. Brush the foil with the olive oil.
2. Place the salmon fillets skin-side down on the baking sheet.
3. Spread 1 tablespoon of pesto on each fillet.
4. Roast the salmon for about 20 minutes, or just until opaque in the center.
5. Serve immediately.

**Cooking tip:** Enjoy a gourmet meal any night of the week by keeping a bag of freshly frozen wild

Alaskan salmon fillets on hand. Look for the kind that are perfectly portioned into individual fillets for easy meal prep—just thaw in the fridge a day or two before needed.

**NUTRITION:** Per Serving (3 ounces): Calories: 182; Total fat: 10g; Protein: 20g; Carbs: 1g; Fiber: 0g; Sugar: 0g; Sodium: 90mg

## BAKED HALIBUT WITH TOMATOES AND WHITE WINE

Preparation Time: 5 minutes

Cooking Time: 15 minutes

Servings: 2-3

### INGREDIENTS:

- 3 tablespoons of extra-virgin olive oil
- 1 Vidalia onion, chopped
- 1 tablespoon minced garlic
- 1 (10-ounce) container grape tomatoes
- ¾ cup dry white wine, divided
- 3 tablespoons capers
- 1½ pounds thick-cut halibut fillet, deboned
- ½ teaspoon dried oregano
- Salt
- Freshly ground black pepper

### DIRECTIONS:

1. Preheat the oven to 350°F.
2. In a pan, heat the olive oil. Add the onion and sauté until browned and softened, 3 to 5 minutes.
3. Add the garlic and cook until fragrant, 1 to 2 minutes.
4. Add the tomatoes and cook for 5 minutes, or until they start to soften. Once the tomatoes start to soften, carefully use a potato masher to crush the tomatoes just enough to release their juices gently.
5. Add ½ cup of the wine to the pan and stir. Cook 2 to 3 minutes until slightly thickened. Stir in the capers.
6. Push the vegetables to the sides of the pan leaving the center of the pan open for the fish. Place the fish in the pan and sprinkle it with the oregano, salt, and pepper, then scoop the tomato mixture over the fish.
7. Pour in the remaining ¼ cup of wine.
8. Place in the oven and bake for about 20 minutes, uncovered, or until the fish flakes easily with a fork or reaches an internal temperature of 145°F. Serve.

**NUTRITION:** Per Serving (4 ounces): Calories: 237; Total fat: 10g; Protein: 24g; Carbs: 6g; Fiber: 1g; Sugar: 2g; Sodium: 166mg

## BAKED COD WITH FENNEL AND KALAMATA OLIVES

Preparation Time: 10 minutes

Cooking Time: 35 minutes

Servings: 2-3

### INGREDIENTS:

- 2 teaspoons extra-virgin olive oil
- 1 fennel bulb, sliced paper thin
- ¼ cup dry white wine
- 1/8 cup freshly squeezed orange juice
- 1 teaspoon freshly ground black pepper
- 4 (4-ounce) cod fillets
- 4 slices fresh orange (with rind)
- ¼ cup Kalamata olives, pitted
- 2 bay leaves

### DIRECTIONS:

1. Preheat the oven to 400°F.
2. Place a pan on medium heat and add the olive oil. Add the fennel and cook, stirring occasionally, until softened, 8 to 10 minutes.
3. Add the wine. Bring it to a simmer and cook for 1 to 2 minutes. Stir in the orange juice and pepper and simmer for 2 minutes more.
4. Remove the pan from the heat and arrange the cod on top of the fennel mixture. Place the orange slices over the fillets. Position the olives and bay leaves around fish.
5. Roast for 20 minutes, or until fish is opaque. The fish is done when it flakes

easily with a fork or reaches an internal temperature of 145°F. Remove the bay leaves prior to serving.

**NUTRITION:** Calories: 186; Total fat: 5g; Protein: 21g; Carbs: 8g; Fiber: 3g; Sugar: 4g; Sodium: 271mg

## SHRIMP, ZUCCHINI AND CHERRY TOMATO SAUCE

Preparation Time: 5 minutes

Cooking Time: 15 minutes

Servings: 2-3

**INGREDIENTS:**

- 2 zucchinis
- 300 shrimp
- 7 cherry tomatoes
- Salt and pepper to taste
- 1 clove garlic

**DIRECTIONS:**

1. Pour the oil in the air fryer, add the garlic clove and diced zucchini.
2. Cook for 15 minutes at 1500C.
3. Add the shrimp and the pieces of tomato, salt, and spices.
4. Cook for another 5 to 10 minutes or until the shrimp water evaporates.

**NUTRITION:** Calories 214.3 Fat 8.6g Carbohydrate 7.8g Sugars 4.8g Protein 27.0g Cholesterol 232.7mg

## MONKFISH WITH OLIVES AND CAPERS

Preparation Time: 25 minutes

Cooking Time: 20 minutes

Servings: 2-3

**INGREDIENTS:**

- 1 monkfish
- 10 cherry tomatoes
- 50 g cailletier olives
- 5 capers

**DIRECTIONS:**

1. Spread aluminum foil inside the air fryer basket and place the monkfish clean and skinless.
2. Add chopped tomatoes, olives, capers, oil, and salt.
3. Set the temperature to 1600C.
4. Cook the monkfish for about 40 minutes.

**NUTRITION:** Calories 404 Fat 29g Carbohydrates 36g Sugars 7g Protein 24g Cholesterol 36mg

## BAKED GARLIC SCALLOPS

Preparation Time: 5-10 min.

Cooking Time: 10 min.

Servings: 2-3

**INGREDIENTS:**

- 5 cloves garlic, minced
- 2 shallots, chopped
- 16 sea scallops, rinsed and drained
- 5 tablespoons butter, melted
- 3 pinches ground nutmeg
- 1 cup bread crumbs
- 4 tablespoons olive oil
- 1/4 cup chopped parsley
- Black pepper (ground) and salt to taste

**DIRECTIONS:**

1. In a mixing bowl, shallots, garlic, melted butter, scallops, salt, nutmeg, and pepper. Combine to mix well with each other.
2. In another bowl, add oil and bread crumbs. Combine to mix well with each other.
3. Place Instant Pot over kitchen platform. Place Air Fryer Lid on top. Press Air Fry, set the temperature to 375°F and set the timer to 5 minutes to preheat. Press "Start" and allow it to preheat for 5 minutes.

4. Take Air Fryer Basket, grease it with some cooking spray. In the basket, add a scallop mixture and top with the crumb mixture.
5. Place the basket in the inner pot of Instant Pot, close Air Fryer Lid on top.
6. Press the "Bake" setting. Set temperature to 390°F and set the timer to 10 minutes.

Press "Start." Cook until the top is light brown.
7. Open Air Fryer Lid after cooking time is over. Serve warm with the parsley on top.

**NUTRITION:** Calories: 407 Fat: 21g Saturated Fat: 2g Trans Fat: 0g Carbohydrates: 28.5g Fiber: 4g Sodium: 358mg Protein: 15g,

## EASY CRAB STICKS

Preparation Time: 5 minutes

Cooking Time: 5 minutes

Servings: 2-3

**INGREDIENTS:**

- Crab sticks (1 package)
- Cooking oil spray (as needed)

**DIRECTIONS:**

1. Take each of the sticks out of the package and unroll it until the stick is flat. Tear the sheets into thirds.
2. Arrange them on the air fryer basket and lightly spritz using cooking spray. Set the timer for 10 minutes.

**Note:** If you shred the crab meat, you can cut the time in half, but they will also easily fall through the holes in the basket.

**NUTRITION:** Calories 285; Fat 12.8 g; Carbohydrates 3.7 g; Protein 38.1 g;

## VINEGAR SPICE PRAWNS

Preparation Time: 5 min.

Cooking Time: 8 min.

Servings: 3-4

**INGREDIENTS:**

- 1 tablespoon ketchup
- 12 prawns, shelled and deveined
- 1 tablespoon white wine vinegar
- ½ teaspoon black pepper
- ½ teaspoon sea salt
- 1 teaspoon chili flakes
- 1 teaspoon chili powder

**DIRECTIONS:**

1. Place Instant Pot over kitchen platform. Place Air Fryer Lid on top. Press Air Fry, set the temperature to 375°F and set the timer to 5 minutes to preheat. Press "Start" and allow it to preheat for 5 minutes.
2. Take Air Fryer Basket, grease it with some cooking spray. In the basket, add all ingredients and combine well.
3. Place the basket in the inner pot of Instant Pot, close Air Fryer Lid on top.
4. Press the "Air Fry" setting. Set temperature to 390°F and set the timer to 8 minutes. Press "Start." Stir mixture halfway down.

5.  Open Air Fryer Lid after cooking time is over. Serve warm.

**NUTRITION:** Calories: 178 Fat: 3.5g Saturated Fat: 1g Trans Fat: 0g Carbohydrates: 9g Fiber: 1g Sodium: 581mg Protein: 21g

## HERBED BAKED SHRIMP

Preparation Time: 5-10 min.

Cooking Time: 10 min.

Servings: 2-3

### INGREDIENTS:

- 1 tablespoon minced garlic
- 2 teaspoons red pepper flakes
- 4 tablespoons butter
- 1 tablespoon lemon juice
- 1 tablespoon chopped chives
- 1 tablespoon minced basil leaves
- 2 tablespoons chicken stock (or white wine)
- 1-pound defrosted shrimp

### DIRECTIONS:

1.  Place Instant Pot over kitchen platform. Place Air Fryer Lid on top. Press Air Fry, set the temperature to 375°F and set the timer to 5 minutes to preheat. Press "Start" and allow it to preheat for 5 minutes.
2.  Take Air Fryer Basket, grease it with some cooking spray. In the basket, add shrimp, butter.
3.  Place the basket in the inner pot of Instant Pot, close Air Fryer Lid on top.
4.  Press the "Bake" setting. Set temperature to 330°F and set the timer to 2 minutes. Press "Start."
5.  Open Air Fryer Lid after cooking time is over. Mix in red pepper flakes and garlic.
6.  Press the "Bake" setting. Set temperature to 330°F and set the timer to 3 minutes. Press "Start." Add other ingredients and combine them.
7.  Press the "Bake" setting. Set temperature to 330°F and set the timer to 5 minutes. Press "Start." Serve warm.

**NUTRITION:** Calories: 233 Fat: 12g Saturated Fat: 2.5g Trans Fat: 0g Carbohydrates: 3g

# CHAPTER 9. POULTRY RECIPES

## THANKSGIVING TURKEY WITH MUSTARD GRAVY

Preparation time: 50 minutes

Cooking time: 45 minutes

Servings: 2-3

### INGREDIENTS:

- 2 teaspoons butter, softened
- 1 teaspoon dried sage
- 2 sprigs rosemary, chopped
- 1 teaspoon salt
- 1/4 teaspoon freshly ground black pepper, or more to taste
- 1 whole turkey breast
- 2 tablespoons turkey broth
- 2 tablespoons whole-grain mustard
- 1 tablespoon butter

### DIRECTIONS:

1. Start by preheating your air fryer to 360-degrees f.
2. To make the rub, combine 2 tablespoons of butter, sage, rosemary, salt, and pepper; mix well to combine and spread it evenly over the surface of the turkey breast.
3. Roast for 20 minutes in an air fryer cooking basket. Flip the turkey breast over and cook for a further 15 to 16 minutes. Now, flip it back over and roast for 12 minutes more.
4. While the turkey is roasting, whisk the other ingredients in a saucepan. After that, spread the gravy all over the turkey breast.
5. Let the turkey rest for a few minutes before carving.

**NUTRITION:** Calories: 415 Fat: 19.4g Fiber: 12.1g Carbs: 31g Protein: 27.1g

## DRY-RUBBED CHICKEN WINGS

Preparation Time: 5 minutes

Cooking Time: 15 minutes

Servings: 2-3

### INGREDIENTS:

- 12 chicken wings
- 1 tsp garlic powder
- 1 tsp chili powder
- 1/2 tsp kosher salt
- 1/2 black pepper, paprika

### DIRECTIONS:

1. Preheat air fryer to 180°C
2. Mix garlic powder, chili powder, paprika, salt and pepper in a large bowl.
3. Rinse and pat every chicken wing dry and toss into a bowl to cover uniformly.
4. Place wings in air fryer crate and cook for 15 minutes, turning at interims.
5. Cool again for an additional 5 minutes.
6. Serve hot.

**NUTRITION:** Calories: 315 Fat: 3.4g Fiber: 7.1g Carbs: 25.7g Protein: 19.1g

## HERBED ROAST CHICKEN

Preparation Time: 35 minutes

Cooking Time: 1 hr. 30 minutes

Servings: 2-3

### INGREDIENTS:

- 1 (3.5 lb.) whole chicken
- 2 tbsp olive oil
- 1 tsp garlic powder
- 1 tsp paprika
- ½ tsp oregano
- Salt and black pepper to taste
- 1 lemon, cut into quarters
- 5 garlic cloves

### DIRECTIONS:

1. In a bowl, combine olive oil, garlic powder, paprika, oregano, salt, and pepper, and mix well to make a paste. Rub the chicken with the paste and stuff lemon and garlic cloves into the cavity.
2. Place the chicken in the air fryer, breast side down, and tuck the legs and wings tips under. Bake for 45 minutes at 360 F. Flip the chicken to breast side up and cook for another 15-20 minutes. Let rest for 5-6 minutes, then carve, and serve.

**NUTRITION:** Calories: 280 Fat: 5.7g Fiber: 12.1g Carbs: 40.7g Protein: 12.9g

## ZAATAR CHICKEN

Preparation Time: 15 minutes

Cooking Time: 20-30 minutes

Servings: 2-3

### INGREDIENTS:

- 4 chicken thighs
- 2 sprigs thyme
- 1 onion, cut into chunks
- 2 1/2 tbsp zaatar
- 1/2 tsp cinnamon
- 2 garlic cloves, smashed
- 1 lemon juice
- 1 lemon zest
- 1/4 cup olive oil
- 1/4 tsp pepper
- 1 tsp salt

### DIRECTIONS:

1. Add oil, lemon juice, lemon zest, cinnamon, garlic, pepper, 2 tbsp zaatar, and salt in a large zip-lock bag and shake well.
2. Add chicken, thyme, and onion to bag and shake well to coat. Place in refrigerator for overnight.
3. Preheat the air fryer to 380 F.
4. Add marinated chicken in air fryer basket and cook at 380 F for 15 minutes.
5. Turn chicken to another side and sprinkle with remaining zaatar spice and cook at 380 F for 15-18 minutes more.
6. Serve and enjoy.

**NUTRITION:** Calories: 399 Fat: 15.7g Fiber: 19.5g Carbs: 67g Protein: 21.1g

## TURKEY LOAF

Preparation Time: 20 minutes

Cooking Time: 40 minutes

Servings: 2-3

### INGREDIENTS:

- 1 egg
- ½ teaspoon dried savory dill

- 2/3 cup walnuts, finely chopped
- 1 ½ lbs. turkey breast, diced
- ½ teaspoon ground allspice
- ¼ teaspoon black pepper
- 1 garlic clove, minced
- 1 tablespoon Dijon mustard
- 1 tablespoon liquid Aminos
- 1 tablespoon tomato paste
- 2 tablespoons parmesan cheese, grated
- 1 tablespoon onion flakes

### DIRECTIONS:

1. Preheat your air fryer to 375-degree Fahrenheit.
2. Grease a baking dish using cooking spray.
3. Whisk dill, egg, tomato paste, liquid aminos, mustard, garlic, allspice, salt, and pepper.
4. Mix well and add diced turkey. Mix again and add cheese, walnuts and onion flakes.
5. Put mixture into baking dish and bake for 40-minutes in air fryer. Serve hot!

**NUTRITION:** Calories: 277 Fat: 5.7g Fiber: 4.51g Carbs: 45.6g Protein: 10.6 g

## CHEESY TURKEY CALZONE

Preparation Time: 20 minutes

Cooking Time: 10-15minutes

Servings: 2-3

### INGREDIENTS:

- 1 free-range egg, beaten
- ¼ cup mozzarella cheese, grated
- 1 cup cheddar cheese, grated
- Cooked turkey, shredded
- 4 tablespoons tomato sauce
- Salt and pepper to taste
- 1 teaspoon thyme
- 1 teaspoon basil
- 1 teaspoon oregano
- 1 package frozen pizza dough

### DIRECTIONS:

1. Roll the pizza dough out into small circles, the same size as a small pizza. Add thyme, oregano, basil into a bowl with tomato sauce and mix well.
2. Pour a small amount of sauce onto your pizza bases and spread across the surface. Add the turkey, and cheese.
3. Brush the edge of dough with beaten egg, then fold over and pinch to seal. Brush the outside with more egg.
4. Place into air fryer and cook at 350-degree Fahrenheit for 10-minutes. Serve warm.

**NUTRITION:** Calories: 265 Fat: 8.5g Fiber: 7.1g Carbs: 39.7g Protein: 12.5 g

## KOREAN CHICKEN WINGS

Preparation Time: 10 minutes

Cooking Time: 15 minutes

Servings: 2-3

**Ingredients:**

- 8 chicken wings
- Salt to taste
- 1 tsp sesame oil
- Juice from half lemon
- ¼ cup sriracha chili sauce
- 1-inch piece ginger, grated
- 1 tsp garlic powder
- 1 tsp sesame seeds

**DIRECTIONS:**

1. Preheat air fryer to 370 F. Grease the air fryer basket with cooking spray.
2. In a bowl, mix salt, ginger, garlic, lemon juice, sesame oil, and chili sauce. Add in the wings and coat them well. Air Fry for 15 minutes, flipping once. Sprinkle with sesame seeds and serve.

**NUTRITION:** Calories: 154 Fat: 2.8g Fiber: 9.1g Carbs: 22.1g Protein: 10.4 g

## COCONUT CHICKEN MEATBALLS

Preparation Time: 30 minutes

Cooking Time: 10-15 minutes

Servings: 2-3

**INGREDIENTS:**

- 1 lb. ground chicken
- 1 ½ tsp sriracha
- 1/2 tbsp soy sauce
- 1/2 tbsp hoisin sauce
- ¼ cup shredded coconut
- 1 tsp sesame oil
- ½ cup fresh cilantro, chopped
- 2 green onions, chopped
- Pepper
- Salt

**DIRECTIONS:**

1. Spray air fryer basket with cooking spray.
2. Add all ingredients into the large bowl and mix until well combined.
3. Make small balls from meat mixture and place into the air fryer basket.
4. Cook at 350 F for 10 minutes. Turn halfway through.
5. Serve and enjoy.

**NUTRITION:** Calories: 241 Fat: 2.8g Fiber: 8.1g Carbs: 21.7g Protein: 11.5 g

## SUNDRIED TOMATO AND GOAT CHEESE TURKEY ROLL

Preparation Time: 15 minutes

Cooking Time: 20 minutes

Servings: 2-3

**INGREDIENTS:**

- 4 fillets of turkey breast
- 4 halves of sun-dried tomatoes
- 200 g goat cheese
- Salt
- Chile

**DIRECTIONS:**

1. Beat the fillets with the meat whisk (to soften to taste). Season with salt, pepper and oil to taste.
2. Place half a slice of tomato and 50 g of goat cheese on each of the fillets.
3. Roll them up and then wrap them in aluminum foil.
4. Arrange the rolls in a pan and bake in the preheated air fryer at 4200F for 20 to 30 minutes.

5. Remove from the air fryer, open the rollers and spread a little butter/margarine on them.
6. Put them back in the pan and back in the air fryer until golden.
7. Serve hot with rice and arugula salad or serve cold with mayonnaise-based sauces.

**NUTRITION:** Calories: 310 Fat: 8.6g Fiber: 12.9g Carbs: 55.9g Protein: 19.5g

## CREOLE CORNISH HEN

Preparation Time: 10 minutes

Cooking Time: 40 minutes

Servings: 2-3

### INGREDIENTS:

- 2 tablespoons olive oil, plus more for spraying
- ½ tablespoon Creole seasoning
- ½ tablespoon garlic powder
- ½ tablespoon onion powder
- ½ tablespoon freshly ground black pepper
- ½ tablespoon paprika
- 2 Cornish hens

### DIRECTIONS:

1. Set to 370 F. Spray a fryer basket lightly with olive oil.
2. In a small bowl, mix together the Creole seasoning, garlic powder, onion powder, pepper, and paprika.
3. Pat the Cornish hens dry and brush each hen all over with the 2 tablespoons of olive oil. Rub each hen with the seasoning mixture.
4. Place the Cornish hens in the fryer basket. Air fry for 15 minutes. Flip the hens over and baste with any drippings collected in the bottom drawer of the air fryer. Lightly spray them with olive oil.
5. Air fry for 15 minutes. Flip the hens back over and cook until a thermometer inserted into the thickest part of the thigh reaches at least 165°F and it's crispy and golden, an additional 5 to 10 minutes.
6. Let the hens rest for 10 minutes before carving.

**NUTRITION:** Calories: 315 Fat: 9.6g Fiber: 12.8g Carbs: 32g Protein: 11g

## CARIBBEAN CHICKEN THIGHS

Preparation Time: 30 minutes

Cooking Time: 10 minutes

Servings: 2-3

### INGREDIENTS:

- Chicken thigh fillets: 3 Lbs., boneless and skinless
- Ground black pepper
- Ground coriander seed: 1 tablespoon
- Salt
- Ground cinnamon: 1 tablespoon
- Cayenne pepper: 1 tablespoon
- Ground ginger: 1 ½ teaspoons
- Ground nutmeg: 1 ½ teaspoons
- Coconut oil: 3 tablespoons

### DIRECTIONS:

1. Take chicken off the packaging and pat dry. To soak up any residual liquid, place on a large baking sheet covered with paper towels. Chicken is salted and peppered on both sides. Let the chicken sit for 30 minutes, so when you go into the air fryer, it isn't that cold.
2. Combine cilantro, cinnamon, cayenne, ginger, and nutmeg in a small bowl. Coat the spice mixture on each piece of chicken and brush both sides with coconut oil.
3. Place four pieces of chicken in your air fryer basket (they shouldn't overlap). Air fry for 10 minutes at 390 degrees F. Remove the chicken from the basket and place it in a safe stove dish, tightly covered with foil.
4. Keep the chicken in the oven to keep it warm until the remaining chicken is done

— repeat the instructions for air frying with the rest of the chicken.

**NUTRITION:** Calories: 276 Fat: 6.4g Fiber: 12.1g Carbs: 56.5g Protein: 13.1g

## QUAIL IN WHITE WINE SAUCE

Preparation Time: 12 hrs.

Cooking Time: 90 minutes

Servings: 2-3

### INGREDIENTS:

- 4 large quail
- 1 bottle of dry white wine
- 1 tsp of sweet paprika
- 1 tsp of hot paprika
- ½ package fresh sage, chopped or 2 tbsp dehydrated sage
- 1 head minced garlic
- ¼ tsp of virgin olive oil
- oz. of butter
- Salt to taste
- 4 rosemary sprigs

### DIRECTIONS:

2. The recipe is very easy; it should only be prepared well in advance.
3. Wash the quail well. Boil salted water in a skillet enough to cover the quail.
4. When the water boils, place the quail in the pan and cover for 5 minutes.
5. Drain and let cool. Put a little minced garlic inside each quail. Place the quail in a large bowl and top with white wine. Add sweet bell pepper, hot pepper, olive oil, and sage. Marinate in the seasoning in the refrigerator for at least 12 hours. Remove the quail from the seasoning and place it in a pan with butter.
6. Take to the preheated air fryer to about 2000F and bake for 90 minutes.
7. Open the oven every 15 minutes and turn the quails and sprinkle with the marinade.

**NUTRITION:** Calories: 319 Fat: 19g Fiber: 16.1g Carbs: 78g Protein: 21.1g

## STUFFED TURKEY BREAST

Preparation Time: 35 minutes

Cooking Time: 30 minutes

Servings: 2-3

### INGREDIENTS:

- 3 lb. of turkey breast
- ¼ lb. of banana with raisins
- 1 ¼ cup of water
- 3 ½ oz. of sugar
- 5 ¼ oz. fresh tamarind
- Chopped parsley, salt and freshly ground black pepper to taste

### DIRECTIONS:

1. Open the turkey breast and place the raisin bananas lengthwise inside. Wrap and tie with string. Wrap in foil and bake in the air fryer, preheated at 4000F for approximately 30 minutes.
2. Remove from the air fryer and, with the help of a fork; check that the inside of the turkey is hot. If not, return it to the air fryer.
3. Discard the shell and core of tamarind.
4. In a saucepan, dilute the sugar in the water, add the pulp of the fruit and simmer for at least 30 minutes or until you get a dense and shiny sauce. Remove from heat and strain.
5. Cut the turkey breast and put it on the plates with the tamarind sauce.

**NUTRITION:** Calories: 310 Fat: 10.6g Fiber: 18.5g Carbs: 71g Protein: 15.9g

## HAWAIIAN ROASTED QUAIL

Preparation Time: 20 minutes

Cooking Time: 30 minutes

Servings: 2-3

### INGREDIENTS:

- 1 cup champagne
- 1 cup of water
- ½ tbsp ground black pepper
- 2 tsp of salt
- 3 tsp of curry
- 3 tsp virgin olive oil
- 3 minced garlic
- 3 ½ tsp lemon vinegar
- 4 medium size Hawaii pineapple slices
- 4 very clean quails washed and dried
- 20 sliced endive leaves

**NUTRITION:** Calories: 287 Fat: 7.5g Fiber: 12.9g Carbs: 45.9g Protein: 18.5 g

### DIRECTIONS:

1. Cut the pineapple curry slices. Reserve.
2. Heat 2 tablespoons of oil in a frying pan and brown the pineapple slices on both sides.
3. Chop them and fill the quail. Tie well Place on the baking sheet. Season with champagne, water, salt, and garlic.
4. Bake in the air fryer for 40 minutes or until golden brown.
5. Arrange the quail on the plates. Add endive and reserve.
6. Mix the vinegar, remaining oil, and pepper. Endive water. Pineapple, rosemary and thyme leaves to decorate.

## CHICKEN SOUP

Preparation time: 30 min

Cooking time: 1 hour

Servings: 2-3

### INGREDIENTS:

- 2 cups of black beans salsa
- 1-pound chicken tenderloins
- 1 teaspoon salt
- 2 teaspoon Mexican spice
- 1 teaspoon ground cumin
- 4 cups of water
- 2 cups of frozen corn
- 4.5-ounce green chilies
- 10-ounce diced tomatoes
- 2 tablespoons fresh coriander
- 10-ounce black beans
- 1 teaspoon black pepper

- Cheese and lime juice for garnishing (optional)

### DIRECTIONS:

1. Rinse the chicken tenderloins. Sprinkle pepper and salt on them before putting them in the crockpot.
2. Put the salsa and the spices. Then cook for 4 hours on low heat.
3. Take out and shred the chicken. Put it back in the crockpot. Add water, additional beans, corn, tomatoes, coriander, and chilies. Cook for 2 more hours.
4. Garnish with cheese and coriander leaves. Add a dash of lime juice and servings.

**NUTRITION:** Servings: 2-32ouces calories: 375kcal carbohydrates: 10g protein: 22g fat: 29g saturated fat: 22g cholesterol: 53mg sodium: 1283mg potassium: 740mg fiber: 2g sugar: 5g vitamin a: 29iu vitamin c: 21mg iron: 3mg

## THANKSGIVING TURKEY WITH MUSTARD GRAVY

Preparation time: 50 minutes

Cooking time: 45 minutes

Servings: 2-3

### Ingredients:

- 2 teaspoons butter, softened
- 1 teaspoon dried sage
- 2 sprigs rosemary, chopped
- 1 teaspoon salt

- 1/4 teaspoon freshly ground black pepper, or more to taste
- 1 whole turkey breast
- 2 tablespoons turkey broth
- 2 tablespoons whole-grain mustard
- 1 tablespoon butter

**Directions:**

1. Start by preheating your air fryer to 360-degrees f.
2. To make the rub, combine 2 tablespoons of butter, sage, rosemary, salt, and pepper; mix well to combine and spread it evenly over the surface of the turkey breast.

3. Roast for 20 minutes in an air fryer cooking basket. Flip the turkey breast over and cook for a further 15 to 16 minutes. Now, flip it back over and roast for 12 minutes more.
4. While the turkey is roasting, whisk the other ingredients in a saucepan. After that, spread the gravy all over the turkey breast.
5. Let the turkey rest for a few minutes before carving.

**Nutrition:** Calories: 415 Fat: 19.4g Fiber: 12.1g Carbs: 31g Protein: 27.1g

## DRY-RUBBED CHICKEN WINGS

Preparation Time: 5 minutes
Cooking Time: 15 minutes
Servings: 2-3
**Ingredients:**
- 12 chicken wings
- 1 tsp garlic powder
- 1 tsp chili powder
- 1/2 tsp kosher salt
- 1/2 black pepper, paprika

**Directions:**
1. Preheat air fryer to 180°C

2. Mix garlic powder, chili powder, paprika, salt and pepper in a large bowl.
3. Rinse and pat every chicken wing dry and toss into a bowl to cover uniformly.
4. Place wings in air fryer crate and cook for 15 minutes, turning at interims.
5. Cool again for an additional 5 minutes.
6. Serve hot.

**Nutrition:** Calories: 315 Fat: 3.4g Fiber: 7.1g

Carbs: 25.7g Protein: 19.1g

## HERBED ROAST CHICKEN

Preparation Time: 35 minutes
Cooking Time: 1 hr. 30 minutes
Servings: 2-3
**Ingredients:**
- 1 (3.5 lb.) whole chicken
- 2 tbsp olive oil
- 1 tsp garlic powder
- 1 tsp paprika
- ½ tsp oregano
- Salt and black pepper to taste
- 1 lemon, cut into quarters
- 5 garlic cloves

**Directions:**
1. In a bowl, combine olive oil, garlic powder, paprika, oregano, salt, and pepper, and mix well to make a paste. Rub the

chicken with the paste and stuff lemon and garlic cloves into the cavity.
2. Place the chicken in the air fryer, breast side down, and tuck the legs and wings tips under. Bake for 45 minutes at 360 F. Flip the chicken to breast side up and cook for another 15-20 minutes. Let rest for 5-6 minutes, then carve, and serve.

**Nutrition:** Calories: 280 Fat: 5.7g Fiber: 12.1g Carbs: 40.7g Protein: 12.9g

## ZAATAR CHICKEN

Preparation Time: 15 minutes
Cooking Time: 20-30 minutes
Servings: 2-3

**Ingredients**:

- 4 chicken thighs
- 2 sprigs thyme
- 1 onion, cut into chunks
- 2 1/2 tbsp zaatar
- 1/2 tsp cinnamon
- 2 garlic cloves, smashed
- 1 lemon juice
- 1 lemon zest
- 1/4 cup olive oil
- 1/4 tsp pepper
- 1 tsp salt

**Directions**:

1. Add oil, lemon juice, lemon zest, cinnamon, garlic, pepper, 2 tbsp zaatar, and salt in a large zip-lock bag and shake well.
2. Add chicken, thyme, and onion to bag and shake well to coat. Place in refrigerator for overnight.
3. Preheat the air fryer to 380 F.
4. Add marinated chicken in air fryer basket and cook at 380 F for 15 minutes.
5. Turn chicken to another side and sprinkle with remaining zaatar spice and cook at 380 F for 15-18 minutes more.
6. Serve and enjoy.

**Nutrition**: Calories: 399 Fat: 15.7g Fiber: 19.5g Carbs: 67g Protein: 21.1g

## SPICY ASIAN CHICKEN

Preparation Time: 10 minutes
Cooking Time: 20 minutes
Servings: 2-3

**Ingredients**:

- 4 chicken thighs, skin-on, and bone-in
- 2 tsp ginger, grated
- 1 lime juice
- 2 tbsp chili garlic sauce
- 1/4 cup olive oil
- 1/3 cup soy sauce

**Directions**:

1. In a large bowl, whisk together ginger, lime juice, chili garlic sauce, oil, and soy sauce.
2. Add chicken in bowl and coat well with marinade and place in the refrigerator for 30 minutes.
3. Place marinated chicken in air fryer basket and cook at 400 F for 15-20 minutes or until the internal temperature of chicken reaches at 165 F. Turn chicken halfway through.
4. Serve and enjoy.

**Nutrition**: Calories: 318 Fat: 6.7g Fiber: 11.5g Carbs: 49.9g Protein: 18.4g

# CHAPTER 10. BEEF, PORK AND LAMB DISHES

## BBQ LAMB

Preparation Time: 90 minutes

Cooking Time: 8 minutes

Servings: 2-3

### INGREDIENTS:

- 4 lbs. boneless leg of lamb, cut into 2-inch chunks
- 2-1/2 tbsps. herb salt
- 2 tbsps. olive oil

### DIRECTIONS:

1. Preheat the PowerXL Air Fryer Grill by selecting air fryer mode
2. Adjust the temperature to 390°F, set Time to 5 minutes
3. Season the meat with salt and olive oil
4. Arrange on the Air fryer baking tray
5. Transfer to the PowerXL Air Fryer Grill
6. Air fry for 15 minutes, flipping halfway through
7. Serve and enjoy
8. Serving Suggestions: serve with marinara sauce
9. Directions: & Cooking Tips: work in batches

**NUTRITION:** Calories: 341kcal, Fat: 16g, Carb: 1g, Proteins: 26g

## LAMB MEATBALLS

Preparation Time: 15minutes

Cooking Time: 8 minutes

Servings: 2-3-2

### INGREDIENTS:

- 1 lb. ground lamb
- 1/2 cup breadcrumbs
- 1 lemon, juiced and zested
- 1/4 cup milk
- 2 egg yolks
- 1 tsp ground cumin
- 1 tsp dried oregano
- 1/2 tsp salt
- 1 tsp ground coriander
- 1/2 tsp black pepper
- 3 garlic cloves, minced
- 1/4 cup fresh parsley, chopped
- 1/2 cup crumbled feta cheese

### DIRECTIONS:

1. Preheat the PowerXL Air Fryer Grill by selecting Broil mode
2. Adjust the temperature to 390°F, set Time to 5 minutes
3. Combine all the Ingredients: in a bowl
4. Form into 12 balls
5. Arrange on the Air fryer baking tray

6. Transfer to the PowerXL Air Fryer Grill
7. Cook for 12 minutes
8. Serve and enjoy
9. Serving Suggestions: Serve with tzatziki sauce

10. Directions: & Cooking Tips: rub olive oil on your hand when forming the meatballs

**NUTRITION:** Calories: 129kcal, Fat: 6.4g, Carb: 4.9g, Proteins: 25g

## GLAZED LAMB CHOPS

Preparation Time: 30 minutes

Cooking Time: 8 minutes

Servings: 2-3

### INGREDIENTS:

- 4 (4-ounce) lamb loin chops
- 1 tbsp Dijon mustard
- 1 tsp honey
- 1/2 tbsp fresh lime juice
- 1/2 tsp olive oil
- Salt and ground black pepper, as required

### DIRECTIONS:

1. Preheat the PowerXL Air Fryer Grill by selecting air fryer mode

2. Adjust the temperature to 3900 F, set Time to 5 minutes
3. Combine all the Ingredients: in a bowl
4. Add the Beef chops and toss to coat
5. Arrange on the Air fryer baking tray
6. Transfer to the PowerXL Air Fryer Grill
7. Air fry for 15 minutes, flipping halfway through
8. Serve and enjoy
9. Serving Suggestions: Serve while still hot
10. Directions: & Cooking Tips: leave to marinate for a few minutes

**NUTRITION:** Calories: 224kcal, Fat: 4g, Carb: 2g, Proteins: 19g

## GARLIC LAMB SHANK

Preparation Time: 15 minutes

Cooking Time: 24 minutes

Servings: 2-3

### INGREDIENTS:

- 17 oz. lamb shanks
- 2 tbsp garlic, peeled and coarsely chopped
- tsp kosher salt
- 1/2 cup chicken stock
- tbsp dried parsley
- 1 tsp dried rosemary
- 4 oz. chive stems, chopped
- 1 tsp butter
- 1 tsp nutmeg
- 1/2 tsp ground black pepper

### DIRECTIONS:

1. Make the cuts in the lamb shank and fill the cuts with the chopped garlic.

2. Sprinkle the lamb shank with the kosher salt, dried parsley, dried rosemary, nutmeg, and ground black pepper.
3. Stir the spices on the lamb shank gently.
4. Preheat the PowerXL Air Fryer Grill by selecting air fry mode.
5. Adjust the temperature to 380°F, set Time to 5 minutes
6. Put the butter, chives, and chicken stock in the air fryer baking tray.
7. Add the lamb shank and air fry the meat for 24 minutes.
8. Serve and enjoy
9. Serving Suggestions: Serve with the cooking liquid
10. Directions: & Cooking Tips: add spices to taste

**NUTRITION:** Calories: 205kcal, Fat: 8.2g, Carb: 3g, Proteins: 28g

## INDIAN MEATBALL WITH LAMB

Preparation Time: 10 minutes

Cooking Time: 14minutes

Servings: 2-3

### INGREDIENTS:

- 1 lb. ground lamb
- 1 garlic clove, minced
- 1 egg
- 1 tbsp butter
- 4 oz. chive stems, grated
- 1/4 tbsp turmeric
- 1/3 tsp cayenne pepper
- 1/4 tsp bay leaf
- 1 tsp ground coriander
- 1 tsp salt
- 1 tsp ground black pepper

### DIRECTIONS:

1. Combine all the Ingredients: together in a bowl
2. Preheat the PowerXL air fryer by selecting the air fry mode
3. Adjust the temperature to 390°F and set Time to 5 minutes
4. Put the butter in the Air fryer baking tray and melt it.
5. Form the meatballs
6. Place them in the air fryer baking tray.
7. Transfer to the PowerXL Air Fryer Grill
8. Cook the dish for 14 minutes.
9. Stir the meatballs twice during the cooking
10. Serving Suggestions: Serve with salad and sauce

**Directions & Cooking Tips:** use an ice-cream scooper to form the balls

**NUTRITION:** Calories: 300kcal, Fat: 13g, Carb: 19g, Proteins: 21g

## ROASTED LAMB

Preparation Time: 60 minutes

Cooking Time: 13 minutes

Servings: 2-3

### INGREDIENTS:

- 2-1/2 pounds lamb leg roast, slits carved
- tbsp olive oil
- garlic cloves, sliced into smaller slithers
- 1 tbsp dried rosemary
- Cracked Himalayan rock salt and cracked peppercorns, to taste

### DIRECTIONS:

1. Make the cuts in the lamb roast and insert them with garlic.
2. Sprinkle the lamb roast with kosher salt, rosemary, and ground black pepper.
3. Brush with oil.
4. Preheat the PowerXL Air Fryer Grill by selecting air fry mode.
5. Adjust the temperature to 380°F, set Time to 5 minutes
6. Place the lamb roast on the Baking Pan
7. Transfer to the PowerXL Air Fryer Grill.
8. Air fry for 1 hour 15 minutes
9. Serve and enjoy

**Serving Suggestions:** serve with mushroom sauce

**Directions: & Cooking Tips:** leave to marinate for some minutes

**NUTRITION:** Calories: 246kcal, Fat: 7g, Carb: 9g, Proteins: 33g

## LAMB GYRO

Preparation Time: 20 minutes

Cooking Time: 8 minutes

Servings: 2-3

### INGREDIENTS:

- 1 pound ground lamb
- 1/2 onion sliced
- 1/4 cup mint, minced
- 1/4 red onion, minced
- 1/8 tsp rosemary
- 1/2 tsp salt
- 1/2 tsp black pepper
- 3/4 cup hummus
- 4 slices pita bread

- 1/2 cucumber, peeled and sliced into thin rounds
- 1 cup romaine lettuce, shredded
- 1 Roma tomato, diced
- 1/4 cup parsley, minced
- 2 cloves garlic, minced
- 12 mint leaves, minced

**DIRECTIONS:**

1. Preheat the PowerXL Air Fryer Grill by selecting broil mode
2. Adjust the temperature to 3700F, set Time to 5 minutes
3. Mix lamb with onions, mint, parsley, garlic, salt, rosemary, and pepper

4. Form into patties
5. Arrange in a lined Air fryer baking tray
6. Transfer to the PowerXL Air Fryer Grill
7. Air fry for 20 minutes, flipping halfway through
8. Assemble the gyro with the remaining Ingredients:
9. Serve and enjoy

**Serving Suggestions:** serve drizzled with tzatziki sauce

**Directions: & Cooking Tips:** mix until well incorporated

**NUTRITION:** Calories: 309kcal, Fat: 14.6g, Carb: 29g, Proteins: 19g

## LEMON LAMB RACK

Preparation Time: 30 minutes

Cooking Time: 5 minutes

Servings: 2-3

**INGREDIENTS:**

- 1/4 cup olive oil
- 3 tbsp garlic, minced
- 1/3 cup dry white wine
- 1 tbsp lemon zest, grated
- 2 tbsps. lemon juice
- 1-1/2 tsp dried oregano, crushed
- 1 tsp thyme leaves, minced
- Salt and black pepper
- 4 lamb rack
- 1 lemon, sliced

**DIRECTIONS:**

1. Preheat the PowerXL Air Fryer Grill by selecting air fryer mode
2. Adjust the temperature to 3700F, set Time to 5 minutes
3. Whisk all the Ingredients: together in a bowl
4. Pour into air fryer baking tray
5. Add the lamb rack
6. Top with lemon
7. Transfer to the PowerXL Air Fryer Grill
8. Air fry for 30 minutes, flipping halfway through
9. Serve and enjoy

**Serving Suggestions:** Serve with the juice

**Directions: & Cooking Tips:** Leave to marinate for a few minutes

**NUTRITION:** Calories: 288kcal, Fat: 7g, Carb: 5g, Proteins: 16g

## STEAK FAJITAS

Preparation Time: 15 minutes

Cooking Time: 15 minutes

Servings: 2-3

**INGREDIENTS:**

**Salsa**

- 1 Onion that has been sliced into strips

- 1 Green bell pepper that has been sliced into strips
- Dried thyme, ½ tsp.
- Mustard powder, ½ tsp.
- Black pepper, 1 tsp.
- Cumin, 1 tsp.
- Dried rosemary, 2 tsp.
- Chili powder, 2 tsp.

- Natural sweetener, 2 packets
- Paprika, 1 tbsp.
- Sea salt, 1 tbsp.
- Lean sirloin steak, 1 pound, cut into strips

**DIRECTIONS:**

1. Place the salt, paprika, sweetener, chili powder, dried rosemary, cumin, pepper, mustard powder, and dried thyme into a bowl and mix well to combine. Take out one teaspoon of this mixture and reserve. Rub the steak slices really well with the spice mixture that you just made. Cover the steak and allow it to marinate until you are ready to cook it.
2. Place a large skillet on the stove and heat to medium-high. Add the onion and pepper to the skillet along with the spice mixture that you set to the side earlier. You need to cook the onion and peppers until they have softened up and the onions turn translucent. Take off heat and place in a bowl. Cover to keep warm.
3. Into the same skillet, add half the seasoned steak and cook for about two minutes per side or until done to your liking. Place cooked steak onto a clean plate and cover until the rest of the steak gets done.
4. Once all the steak strips are done, add everything back into the skillet and warm everything up for a few minutes. Spoon onto plates and enjoy.

**NUTRITION:** Calories: 663 Fat: 22.1 g Protein: 104.7 Carb: 6 g

## TACO BEEF

Preparation Time: 15 minutes

Cooking Time: 8 hours

Servings: 2-3

**INGREDIENTS:**

- Chipotle pepper in adobo sauce, minced, 1
- Minced garlic, 5 cloves
- Chili powder, 2 tsp.
- Small white onion, diced, 1
- Chuck's tender roast, 2 lb.
- Tomato paste, 2 tbsp.
- Beef broth, low sodium, 1 cup
- Paprika, ½ tsp.
- Cumin, 1 tsp.
- Olive oil, 2 tsp.

**DIRECTIONS:**

1. Place paprika, cumin, and chili powder into a small bowl and mix everything together. Rub this mixture into the chuck roast. Make sure that you cover the chuck roast well.
2. Set a large pan on top of the stove and warm it to medium-high. Add in the olive oil and let it get hot. Place beef into the skillet and sear for two minutes. Turn the roast and sear every side. Take the beef out of the skillet and put into the bottom of slow cooker.
3. Add the diced onion into the skillet you seared the beef in and cook for three minutes until onions become soft and translucent. Mix in the garlic, cooking until fragrant. Pour the beef broth into the skillet and scrape with a wooden spoon to deglaze the pan.
4. Add the minced chipotle and tomato paste into the skillet and using a whisk, stir until everything is combined. Allow the mixture to come up to a boil and then turn the heat down until it simmers. Let it simmer for five minutes, or until it has thickened. Take off heat and pour over beef in bottom of slow cooker.

5. Place lid on slow cooker and set on low. Cook for eight hours until the beef will shred easily with a fork.
6. When beef is done, take it out of the cooker and shred it up. Mix it back into the juices so that it is well coated.

7. Use as you would any meat mixture in your favorite Mexican dishes or eat as is.

**NUTRITION:** Calories: 292 Fat: 11.1 g Protein: 42.3 g Carb: 4 g

## CHIPOTLE SHREDDED BEEF

Preparation Time: 10 minutes

Cooking Time: 6 hours

Servings: 2-3

**INGREDIENTS:**

- 1 (7.5-ounce) can chipotle peppers in adobo sauce
- 1½ tablespoons apple cider vinegar
- 1 tablespoon ground cumin
- 1 tablespoon dried oregano
- Juice of 1 lime
- 2 pounds Beef shoulder, trimmed of excess fat

**DIRECTIONS:**

1. Puree the chipotle peppers and adobo sauce using the blender, apple cider vinegar, cumin, oregano, and lime juice.
2. Place the Beef shoulder in the slow cooker, and pour the sauce over it.
3. Cover the slow cooker, and cook on low for 6 hours.
4. The finished Beef should shred easily. Use two forks to shred the Beef in the slow cooker. If there is any additional sauce, allow the Beef to cook on low for 20 minutes more to absorb the remaining liquid.

**NUTRITION:** Per Serving (½ cup Beef): Calories: 260; Total fat: 11g; Protein: 20g; Carbs: 5g; Fiber: 2g; Sugar: 2g; Sodium: 705mg

## ONE-PAN BEEF CHOPS WITH APPLES AND RED ONION

Preparation Time: 10 minutes

Cooking Time: 15 minutes

Servings:

**INGREDIENTS:**

- 2 teaspoons extra-virgin olive oil, divided
- 4 boneless center-cut thin Beef chops
- 2 small apples, thinly sliced
- 1 small red onion, thinly sliced
- 1 cup low-sodium chicken broth
- 1 teaspoon Dijon mustard
- 1 teaspoon dried sage
- 1 teaspoon dried thyme

**DIRECTIONS:**

1. Place a large nonstick frying pan over high heat and add 1 teaspoon of olive oil. When the oil is hot, add the Beef chops and reduce the heat to medium. Sear the chops for 3 minutes on one side, flip, and sear the other side for 3 minutes, 6 minutes total. Put the chops by the side.
2. In the same pan, add the remaining 1 teaspoon of olive oil. Add the apples and onion. Cook for 5 minutes or until tender, stirring frequently to prevent burning.
3. While the apples and onion cook, mix together the broth and Dijon mustard in a small bowl.
4. Add the sage and thyme to the pan and stir to coat the onion and apples. Stir in the broth mixture and return the Beef chops to the pan. Cover the pan and simmer for 10 to 15 minutes.
5. Let Beef chops rest for 2 minutes before cutting.

**NUTRITION:** Per Serving (1 Beef chop): Calories: 234; Total fat: 11g; Protein: 20g; Carbs: 13g; Fiber: 3g; Sugar: 9g; Sodium: 290mg

## SLOW COOKER BEEF WITH RED PEPPERS AND PINEAPPLE

Preparation Time: 10 minutes Cooking Time: 5 hours

Servings: 2-3

### INGREDIENTS:

- ¼ cup low-sodium soy sauce or Bragg Liquid Aminos
- Juice of ½ lemon
- 1 teaspoon garlic powder
- 1 teaspoon ground cumin
- ½ teaspoon cayenne pepper
- ¼ teaspoon ground coriander
- 1½ pounds boneless Beef tenderloin
- 2 red bell peppers, thinly sliced
- 2 (20-ounce) cans pineapple chunks in 100% natural juice or water, drained

### DIRECTIONS:

1. In a small bowl, mix together the soy sauce, lemon juice, garlic powder, cumin, cayenne pepper, and coriander.
2. Place the Beef tenderloin in the slow cooker and add the red bell pepper slices. Cover with the pineapple chunks and their juices. Pour the soy sauce mixture on top.
3. Cover the slow cooker and turn on low for about 5 hours.
4. Shred the Beef with a fork and tongs and continue to cook on low for 20 minutes more, or until juices are absorbed.
5. Serve and enjoy!

**NUTRITION:** Per Serving (3 ounces): Calories: 131; Total fat: 2g; Protein: 17g; Carbs: 11g; Fiber: 2g; Sugar: 8g; Sodium: 431mg

## CREAMY BEEF STROGANOFF WITH MUSHROOMS

Preparation Time: 10 minutes

Cooking Time: 15 minutes

Servings: 2-3

### INGREDIENTS:

- Nonstick cooking spray
- 1½ pounds extra-lean beef sirloin, cut into ½-inch strips
- 1 teaspoon extra-virgin olive oil
- 1 medium onion, chopped
- ½ pound mushrooms, sliced
- 2 tablespoon whole-wheat flour
- 1 cup low-sodium beef broth
- 1 cup water
- 1 teaspoon Worcestershire sauce
- ½ teaspoon dried thyme
- ½ teaspoon dried dill
- ½ cup low-fat plain Greek yogurt
- 2 tablespoons finely chopped fresh parsley, for garnish

### DIRECTIONS:

1. Coat a medium pan with the cooking spray and place over medium-high heat. Add the beef. Cook, stirring frequently, until browned, about 5 minutes. Transfer to a bowl and set aside.
2. In the same pan, heat the olive oil over medium-high heat. Add the onion and cook until tender, 1 to 2 minutes.
3. Add the mushrooms and cook until tender, about 3 minutes.
4. Mix in the flour and stir to coat the onion and mushrooms.
5. Stir in the broth, water, Worcestershire sauce, thyme, dill. Bring to a boil, cover the pan, and cook for about 10 minutes, stirring frequently.
6. Stir in the yogurt. Mix in the beef. Serve, garnished with the parsley.

**NUTRITION:** Per Serving (4 ounces): Calories: 351; Total fat: 9g; Protein: 31g; Carbs: 30g; Fiber: 5g; Sugar: 5g; Sodium: 418mg

## ITALIAN BEEF SANDWICHES

Preparation Time: 10 minutes

Cooking Time: 7 hours

Servings: 2-3

**INGREDIENTS:**

- 1 cup water
- 1 tablespoon balsamic vinegar
- ¾ teaspoon garlic powder
- ¾ teaspoon onion powder
- 1½ teaspoons dried parsley
- ¾ teaspoon dried oregano
- ¼ teaspoon dried thyme
- ½ teaspoon dried basil
- ¼ teaspoon freshly ground black pepper
- 1½ pounds boneless beef chuck roast, fat trimmed
- 1 medium onion, sliced
- 1 red bell pepper, cut into strips
- 6 sprouted-grain hot dog buns or sandwich thins
- 1 (16-ounce) jar pepperoncini (optional)

**DIRECTIONS:**

1. In a small bowl mix together the water, balsamic vinegar, garlic powder, onion powder, parsley, oregano, thyme, basil, and black pepper.
2. Place the beef in the slow cooker and add the onion and bell pepper.
3. Pour the sauce over the roast. Cover the slow cooker and cook on low for 7 hours. The meat should be tender and cooked through.
4. Carefully transfer the roast to a cutting board.
5. Thinly slice the roast.
6. Toast the buns or sandwich thins.
7. Layer each bun with the beef and top with the au jus, pepper, and onion. Serve with pepperoncini (if using).

Nutrition: Per Serving (1 sandwich): Calories: 351; Total fat: 9g; Protein: 31g; Carbs: 30g; Fiber: 5g; Sugar: 5g; Sodium: 418mg

## FLAVORFUL BEEF MEATBALLS

Preparation Time: 10 minutes

Cooking Time: 5 minutes

Servings: 2-3

**INGREDIENTS:**

- 2 eggs, lightly beaten
- 2 tbsp capers
- 1/2 lb. ground Beef
- 3 garlic cloves, minced
- 2 tbsp fresh mint, chopped
- 1/2 tbsp cilantro, chopped
- 2 tsp red pepper flakes, crushed
- 1 1/2 tbsp butter, melted
- 1 tsp kosher salt

**DIRECTIONS:**

1. Preheat the air fryer to 395 F.
2. Add all ingredients into the mixing bowl and mix until well combined.
3. Spray air fryer basket with cooking spray.
4. Make small balls from meat mixture and place into the air fryer basket.
5. Cook meatballs for 10 minutes. Shake basket halfway through.
6. Serve and enjoy.

**NUTRITION:** Calories 159 Fat 8.7 g Carbohydrates 1.9 g Sugar 0.3 g Protein 18.1 g Cholesterol 135 mg

## CRUMBLY BEEF MEATBALLS

Preparation Time: 8 minutes

Cooking Time: 10 minutes

Servings: 2-3

### INGREDIENTS:

- 2 lbs. of ground beef
- 3 large eggs
- 1-1/4 cup panko breadcrumbs
- 1/4 cup chopped fresh parsley
- 1 tsp. dried oregano
- 1/4 cup grated Parmigianino Reggiano
- 1 small clove garlic chopped
- salt and pepper to taste
- 1 tsp. vegetable oil

### DIRECTIONS:

1. Thoroughly mix beef with eggs, crumbs, parsley, and rest of the ingredients.
2. Make small meatballs out of this mixture and place them in the basket.
3. Place the basket inside the Air Fryer toaster oven and close the lid.
4. Select the Air Fry mode at 350°F temperature for 13 minutes.
5. Toss the meatballs after 5 minutes and resume cooking.
6. Serve fresh.

**NUTRITION:** Calories: 221 Cal Protein: 25.1 g Carbs: 11.2 g Fat: 16.5 g

## STEAK NUGGETS

Preparation Time: 10 minutes

Cooking Time: 8 minutes

Servings: 2-3

### INGREDIENTS:

- 1 lb. beef steak, cut into chunks
- 1 large egg, lightly beaten
- 1/2 cup Beef rind, crushed
- 1/2 cup parmesan cheese, grated
- 1/2 tsp salt

### DIRECTIONS:

1. Add egg in a small bowl.
2. In a shallow bowl, mix together Beef rind, cheese, and salt.
3. Dip each steak chunk in egg then coat with Beef rind mixture and place on a plate. Place in refrigerator for 30 minutes.
4. S pray air fryer basket with cooking spray.
5. Preheat the air fryer to 400 F.
6. Place steak nuggets in air fryer basket and cook for 15-18 minutes or until cooked. Shake after every 4 minutes.
7. Serve and enjoy.

**NUTRITION:** Calories 609 Fat 38 g Carbohydrates 2 g Sugar 0.4 g Protein 63 g Cholesterol 195 mg

## BACON JALAPENO POPPERS

Preparation Time: 10 minutes

Cooking Time: 8 minutes

Servings: 2-3

### INGREDIENTS:

- 10 jalapeno peppers, cut in half and remove seeds
- 1/3 cup cream cheese, softened
- 5 turkey bacon strips, cut in half

### DIRECTIONS:

1. Preheat the air fryer to 370 F.
2. Stuff cream cheese into each jalapeno half.
3. Wrap each jalapeno half with half bacon strip and place in the air fryer basket.
4. Cook for 6-8 minutes.
5. Serve and enjoy.

**NUTRITION:** Calories 83 Fat 7.4 g Carbohydrates 1.3 g Sugar 0.5 g Protein 2.8 g Cholesterol 9 mg

## PEPPERONI CHIPS

Preparation Time: 2 minutes

Cooking Time: 8 minutes

Servings: 2-3

### INGREDIENTS:

- 6 oz pepperoni slices

### DIRECTIONS:

1. Place one batch of pepperoni slices in the air fryer basket.
2. Cook for 8 minutes at 360 F.
3. Cook remaining pepperoni slices using same steps.
4. Serve and enjoy.

**NUTRITION:** Calories 51 Fat 1 g Carbohydrates 2 g Sugar 1.3 g Protein 0 g Cholesterol 0 mg

## CHEESE BACON JALAPENO POPPERS

Preparation Time: 10 minutes

Cooking Time: 5 minutes

Servings: 2-3

### INGREDIENTS:

- 10 fresh jalapeno peppers, cut in half and remove seeds
- 2 turkey bacon slices, cooked and crumbled
- 1/4 cup cheddar cheese, shredded
- 6 oz cream cheese, softened

### DIRECTIONS:

1. In a bowl, combine together bacon, cream cheese, and cheddar cheese.
2. Stuff each jalapeno half with bacon cheese mixture.
3. Spray air fryer basket with cooking spray.
4. Place stuffed jalapeno halved in air fryer basket and cook at 370 F for 5 minutes.
5. Serve and enjoy.

**NUTRITION:** Calories 195 Fat 17.3 g Carbohydrates 3.2 g Sugar 1 g Protein 7.2 g Cholesterol 52 mg

## AIR FRY BACON

Preparation Time: 5 minutes

Cooking Time: 5 minutes

Servings: 2-3

### INGREDIENTS:

- 11 turkey bacon slices

### DIRECTIONS:

1. Place half bacon slices in air fryer basket.
2. Cook at 400 F for 10 minutes.
3. Cook remaining half bacon slices using same steps.
4. Serve and enjoy.

**NUTRITION:** Calories 103 Fat 7.9 g Carbohydrates 0.3 g Sugar 0 g Protein 7 g Cholesterol 21 mg

## BEEF STUFFED DUMPLINGS

Preparation Time: 15 minutes

Cooking Time: 12 minutes

Servings: 2-3

### INGREDIENTS:

- 1 tsp. canola oil
- cups chopped book Choy
- 1 tbsp. chopped fresh ginger
- 1 tbsp. chopped garlic
- oz. ground Beef
- 1/4 tsp. crushed red pepper
- 18 dumpling wrappers
- Cooking spray
- tbsp. rice vinegar
- tsp. lower-sodium soy sauce
- 1 tsp. toasted sesame oil
- 1/2 tsp. packed light Sugar
- 1 tbsp. finely chopped scallions

**DIRECTIONS:**

1. In a greased skillet, sauté bok choy for 8 minutes, then add ginger and garlic. Cook for 1 minute.
2. Transfer the bok choy to a plate.
3. Add Beef and red pepper then mix well. Place the dumpling wraps on the working surface and divide the Beef fillings on the dumpling wraps.
4. Wet the edges of the wraps and pinch them together to seal the filling.
5. Place the dumpling in the Air Fryer basket.
6. Set the Air Fryer basket inside the Air Fryer toaster oven and close the lid.
7. Select the Air Fry mode at 375°F temperature for 12 minutes.
8. Flip the dumplings after 6 minutes then resume cooking.
9. Serve fresh.

**NUTRITION:** Calories: 172 Cal Protein: 2.1 g Carbs: 18.6 g Fat: 10.7 g

## CRUNCHY BACON BITES

Preparation Time: 5 minutes

Cooking Time: 5 minutes

Servings: 2-3

**INGREDIENTS:**

- 4 turkey bacon strips, cut into small pieces
- 1/2 cup Beef rinds, crushed
- 1/4 cup hot sauce

**DIRECTIONS:**

1. Add bacon pieces in a bowl.
2. Add hot sauce and toss well.
3. Add crushed Beef rinds and toss until bacon pieces are well coated.
4. Transfer bacon pieces in air fryer basket and cook at 350 F for 10 minutes.
5. Serve and enjoy.

**NUTRITION:** Calories 112 Fat 9.7 g Carbohydrates 0.3 g Sugar 0.2 g Protein 5.2 g Cholesterol 3 mg

## BACON POPPERS

Preparation Time: 10 minutes

Cooking Time: 8 minutes

Servings: 2-3

**INGREDIENTS:**

- strips turkey bacon, crispy cooked
- Dough:
- 2/3 cup water
- tbsp. butter
- 1 tbsp. bacon fat
- 1 tsp. kosher salt
- 2/3 cup all-purpose flour
- eggs
- oz. Cheddar cheese, shredded
- ½ cup jalapeno peppers
- A pinch pepper
- A pinch black pepper

**DIRECTIONS:**

1. Whisk butter with water and salt in a skillet over medium heat. Stir in flour, then stir cook for about 3 minutes.
2. Transfer this flour to a bowl, then whisk in eggs and rest of the ingredients.
3. Fold in bacon and mix well. Wrap this dough in a plastic sheet and refrigerate for 30 minutes. Make small balls out of this dough.
4. Place these bacon balls the Air Fryer toaster oven and close the lid.
5. Select the Air Fry mode at 390°F temperature for 15 minutes. Flip the balls after 7 minutes then resume cooking. Serve warm.

**NUTRITION:** Calories: 240 Cal Protein: 14.9 g Carbs: 7.1 g Fat: 22.5 g

# CHAPTER 11. DESSERTS

## EASY RICE PUDDING

Preparation Time: 5 minutes

Cooking Time: 2 hours and 30 minutes on high

Servings: 2-3

### INGREDIENTS:

- cup of cooked brown rice
- 1 teaspoon of vanilla extract
- cups of rice/almond milk
- Raw honey, to taste
- ¼ cup of cranberries

### DIRECTIONS:

1. Stir together the rice, vanilla extract, and rice milk into the slow cooker pot.
2. Set the slow cooker on HIGH for 2 ½ hours or LOW for 4-5 hours.
3. To serve, stir in a little honey and top with cranberries.

**NUTRITION:** Calories: 106 Protein: 2g Carbohydrates: 20g Fat: 2g Sugar: 8g Sodium: 80mg Potassium: 89mg Phosphorus: 51mg Calcium: 236mg Fiber: 2g

## ALMOND STRAWBERRY CHIA SEED PUDDING

Preparation Time: 10 minutes + 4 hours to chill

Cooking Time: 0 minutes

Servings: 2-3

### INGREDIENTS:

- 2 cups almond milk
- 1 (16 ounce) package fresh strawberries, hulled
- ½ cup of chia seeds
- ¼ cup of honey
- 1 tsp. vanilla extract

### DIRECTIONS:

1. In a blender, purée the almond milk and strawberries until smooth; pour them into a bowl. In the strawberry puree, stir the chia seeds, butter, and vanilla extract.
2. Cover the bowl with a wrap of plastic and freeze it for 4 hours until set.

**NUTRITION:** 209 calories; protein 3.7g; carbohydrates 37.2g; fat 6.3g; sodium 84.9mg

## BLUEBERRY MUFFINS

Preparation Time: 7 minutes

Cooking Time: 18 minutes

Servings: 2-3

### INGREDIENTS:

- 1¾ cups whole flour
- 1/3 cup stevia
- 2½ teaspoons baking powder
- ½ teaspoon salt
- ¾ cup milk
- 1 egg, lightly beaten
- 1/3 cup butter, softened
- 1 cup blueberries, fresh or frozen

### DIRECTIONS

1. Heat oven to 400 degrees
2. In a medium bowl, combine salt, baking powder, stevia and flour then set aside.
3. In a large bowl, beat butter and stevia until creamy; add egg and milk.
4. Add flour mixture to butter mixture and stir until the dry ingredients are moistened

and a few lumps remain; fold in blueberries.
5. Spoon batter into twelve greased muffin cups; bake at 400 degrees for 18 minutes, or until a toothpick can be inserted in the center and come out clean.

**NUTRITION:** Calories 162.8 Total Fat 3.4g Total Carbohydrate 11.2g Protein 7.5g

## CHOCO FROSTY

Preparation Time: 5 minutes

Cooking Time: 5 minutes

Servings: 2-3

### INGREDIENTS:

- 1 tsp. vanilla
- 8 drops liquid stevia
- 2 tbsp. unsweetened cocoa powder
- 1 tbsp. almond butter
- 1 cup heavy cream

### DIRECTIONS:

1. Add all ingredients into the mixing bowl and beat with immersion blender until soft peaks form.
2. Place in refrigerator for 30 minutes.
3. Add frosty mixture into the piping bag and pipe in serving glasses.
4. Serve and enjoy.

**NUTRITION:** Calories 240 Fat 25 g Carbohydrates 4 g Sugar 3 g Protein 3 g Cholesterol 43 mg

## CHEESECAKE FAT BOMBS

Preparation Time: 10 minutes

Cooking Time: 5 minutes

Servings: 2-3

### INGREDIENTS:

- 8 oz. cream cheese
- 1 ½ tsp. vanilla
- 2 tbsp. erythritol
- 4 oz. coconut oil
- 4 oz. heavy cream

### DIRECTIONS:

1. Add all ingredients into the mixing bowl and beat using immersion blender until creamy.
2. Pour batter into the mini cupcake liner and place in refrigerator until set.
3. Serve and enjoy.

**NUTRITION:** Calories 90 Fat 9.8 g Carbohydrates 1.4 g Sugar 0.1 g Protein 0.8 g Cholesterol 17

## MATCHA ICE CREAM

Preparation Time: 5 minutes

Cooking Time: 5 minutes

Servings: 2-3

### INGREDIENTS:

- ½ tsp. vanilla
- 2 tbsp. swerve
- 1 tsp. matcha powder
- 1 cup heavy whipping cream

### DIRECTIONS:

1. Add all ingredients into the glass jar.
2. Seal jar with lid and shake for 4-5 minutes until mixture double.
3. Place in refrigerator for 3-4 hours.
4. Servings chilled and enjoy.

**NUTRITION:** Calories 215 Fat 22 g Carbohydrates 3.8 g Sugar 0.2 g Protein 1.2 g Cholesterol 82 mg

## MOIST AVOCADO BROWNIES

Preparation Time: 10 minutes

Cooking Time: 35 minutes

Servings: 2-3

### INGREDIENTS:

- 2 avocados, mashed
- 2 eggs
- 1 tsp. baking powder
- 2 tbsp. swerve
- 1/3 cup chocolate chips, melted
- 4 tbsp. coconut oil, melted
- 2/3 cup unsweetened cocoa powder

### DIRECTIONS:

1. Preheat the oven to 325 f.
2. In a mixing bowl, mix together all dry ingredients.
3. In another bowl, mix together avocado and eggs until well combined.
4. Slowly add dry mixture to the wet along with melted chocolate and coconut oil. Mix well.
5. Pour batter in greased baking pan and bake for 30-35 minutes.
6. Slice and serve.

**NUTRITION:** Calories 207 Fat 18 g Carbohydrates 11 g Sugar 3.6 g Protein 3.8 g Cholesterol 38 mg

## MIX BERRY SORBET

Preparation Time: 10 minutes
Cooking Time: 5 minutes

Servings: 2-3

### INGREDIENTS:

- ½ cup raspberries, frozen
- ½ cup blackberries, frozen
- 1 tsp. liquid stevia
- 6 tbsp. water

### DIRECTIONS:

1. Add all ingredients into the blender and blend until smooth.
2. Pour blended mixture into the container and place in refrigerator until harden.
3. Servings chilled and enjoy.

**NUTRITION:** Calories 63 Fat 0.8 g Carbohydrates 14 g Sugar 6 g Protein 1.7 g Cholesterol 0 mg

# 21-DAY MEAL PLAN

| 21 DAYS | BREAKFAST | LUNCH | DINNER |
|---|---|---|---|
| Day 1 | Lemon, Mint & Cucumber Infused Water | Mango & Ginger Infused Water | Key Lime Tea |
| Day 2 | Citrus & Mint Infused Water | Lavender & Blueberry Infused Water | Strawberry Juice |
| Day 3 | Pineapple and Mango Water | Pina Colada Infused Water | Grape Juice |
| Day 4 | Honeydew & Kiwi Infused Water | Orange, Strawberry & Mint Infused Water | Mango Juice |
| Day 5 | Sweet and Sour Lychee Infused Water | Watermelon Juice | Apple & Kale Juice |
| Day 6 | Kiwi and Kale Detox Water | Ginger Tea | Watermelon and Strawberries Drink |
| Day 7 | Watermelon and Lemon Water | Orange Juice | Clear Vegetable Stock |
| Day 8 | Piña Colada Smoothie | Squash Soup | Blueberry and Spinach Smoothie |
| Day 9 | Green Mango Smoothie | Creamy Avocado Soup | Broccoli Purée |
| Day 10 | Banana Almond Smoothie | Celery Soup | Easy Chocolate and Orange Pudding |
| Day 11 | Protein Spinach Shake | Cauliflower Soup | Herbed Chicken Purée |
| Day 12 | Fresh Lemon Cream Shake | Avocado Milk Whip | Matcha Mango Smoothie |
| Day 13 | Avocado Banana Smoothie | Banana and Kale Smoothie | Ricotta Peach Fluff |
| Day 14 | Banana Cherry Smoothie | Beef Purée | Simple Applesauce |
| Day 15 | Best Chocolate Porridge | No-Bake Peanut Butter Protein Bites and Dark Chocolate | Strawberries with Whipped Yogurt |
| Day 16 | Chocolate Chia Pudding | Egg White Scramble | Gazpacho |

| Day 17 | Delicious Mugastrone | Ham & Swiss Eggs | Cream of Chicken Soup |
| Day 18 | Lemon-Blackberry Frozen Yogurt | Peanut Butter Cup Smoothies | Mushroom Soup with Brie |
| Day 19 | Creamy Cauliflower Dish | Berry Cheesecake Smoothies | Carrot Pudding |
| Day 20 | Beetroot and Butterbean Hummus | Tropical Porridge | Fancy Scrambled Eggs |
| Day 21 | Raisin and Oats Mug Cakes | Porridge with Berries | Yogurt Crème Brulee Custard |

# CONCLUSION

Maintaining motivation after undergoing gastric sleeve surgery for weight reduction and incorporating exercise can prove to be challenging. To sustain your motivation, consider the following tips:

Many individuals encounter a plateau in their weight loss journey after gastric sleeve surgery, unsure of when to stop or how to prevent becoming underweight or anorexic. It's essential to establish a healthy weight range, such as 150 to 160 pounds, allowing yourself a 10-pound window to avoid fixating on a specific number. This approach alleviates pressure and helps maintain a safe weight zone. When healthy habits start to slip, motivate yourself with positive self-talk. You won't always have someone to accompany you to the gym or remind you of your routines. If you deviate from your plan, don't justify it; instead, address it and avoid falling into a pattern of poor practices. Similarly, when a short vacation extends into weeks or even months due to various reasons, it's crucial to maintain a positive mindset. Establish a resilient mental attitude that propels you to action, even in the face of challenges.

Remember that gastric sleeve surgery is a tool, not an all-encompassing weight loss solution. Rapid initial weight loss can lead to confusion about next steps, resulting in relapses into old habits. Recognize that a healthy lifestyle is a consistent process rather than a race. Post-surgery, monotony can set in with repetitive meals, exercises, and routines. Combat this by experimenting with new recipes from helpful websites and exploring diverse physical activities. Engaging in activities you enjoy, whether it's yoga, swimming, or other alternatives, keeps you active without relying solely on traditional workouts. Confront the habit of keeping unhealthy snacks within easy reach. Remove such temptations from your sight to reduce impulsive eating. If completely discarding them isn't possible, hide them away and place healthier options prominently visible. Find an accountability partner to help you stay on track and curb unhealthy behaviors. Honesty about your patterns and health is essential. Develop a solid meal plan, acquire nutritious foods, exercise consistently, and make these actions habitual. Initially, any new action is challenging, but repetition makes it easier. As you shed weight, movement becomes more comfortable and enjoyable. Silence your inner critic by repeating positive affirmations daily and avoiding comparisons with others. Recognize that each weight loss journey is unique, with specific goals to achieve.

Avoid overwhelming yourself with the perception of arduous tasks. Present your tasks as manageable steps toward your goals. Your weight loss surgery is a practical means of shedding excess weight, but it's not a magical solution. Weight loss plateaus or minor regains are normal; stay prepared for challenges and continue looking ahead. Acknowledge your accomplishments with non-food rewards like a massage or relaxing bath. Transform your surroundings to support your new lifestyle by eliminating tempting foods and placing workout gear in sight. Immediately following surgery, weight loss is rapid, but it slows over time. Practice patience and understand that your commitment to a healthier lifestyle is a lifelong journey. There will be tough days post-surgery, but remember, this surgery marks the beginning of your path to a healthier life. Stay motivated by seeking happiness and success in activities that resonate with you.

Made in the USA
Las Vegas, NV
27 October 2023

79727369R00059